EVER WISH YOU GOT HIT BY A TRUCK?

EVER WISH YOU GOT HIT *by a* TRUCK?

A WOMAN'S MANUAL *for* BRAVELY CHANGING LANES *at* ANY AGE

JENNIFER CROWLEY

HOUNDSTOOTH
PRESS

EVER WISH YOU GOT HIT BY A TRUCK?
A Woman's Manual for Bravely Changing Lanes at Any Age

ISBN   978-1-5445-2176-3 *Paperback*
   978-1-5445-2175-6 *Ebook*

For my parents, my son, and the women of the
world who just need a little push.

CONTENTS

INTRODUCTION

It felt like I was already failing at everything when I went on to make one of the biggest mistakes of my life. I was 40 and my marriage was falling apart, I was struggling to be a good mom, and my demanding job was swallowing me whole. I should have opened up to my family and friends and gathered them around me to help me move forward.

Instead, I chose to go it alone. I suffered and hid my not-so-perfect parts from everyone, which prevented me from finding the strength to make the changes I so obviously needed to make. I let my fear and feelings of inadequacy keep me from connecting in a meaningful way with the people who would build me back up and support me when I needed them most.

As a result, I stayed in that isolated place for far too long. It was such a state of sorrow that it mentally and physically took its toll. Holding myself in unhappiness unnecessarily prolonged my pain, and I want to save you from suffering in the same way.

It doesn't matter if you've just begun to notice that your life seems lackluster or know deep within you that something specific needs to change. Living a life that is less than what you want wears on you. Your ability to get up and face the day with enthusiasm and a smile begins to fade, and the people around you can see that your light has dimmed.

Feeling powerless or stuck makes it that much worse. Frustration slowly invades the space that holds your joy and spark, and it digs into your fears. You start questioning yourself and doubting your ability to make changes, thinking things like, "What if I'm not strong enough?" or "What if I'm too old?" and even "I wouldn't know how to get started."

Women today have more anxiety and feel less happy than in previous generations. The model for female success is overflowing with responsibilities, and women are leading more jam-packed lives than ever. Many are exhausted, feel hopeless, and lack the confidence or ability to put their happiness first. It never feels like the right time to change or make things different, so we do nothing.

As women, we convince ourselves it's easier to stay where we are and keep doing what we're doing. We stick it out and resign ourselves to the thought that struggle is simply a part of life, and this is "just the way it is." Some of us secretly hope something will come along and change our life for us, or even put us out of our misery, like being hit by a truck, or some other calamity.

Staying in a career, relationship, or any situation you know deep down doesn't serve you will keep you from being truly fulfilled. Regardless of what you've been through or have already tried, you must decide that you're worthy of your own effort. Life is too short and too uncertain to have an existence that doesn't feel like it's entirely yours.

I told myself, "It's not supposed to be this hard" as I thought about my personal and professional worlds wound together, and I finally made the decision to leave my 20-year career and revamp my life at the age of 45. My goal was to gain control of my time and find a way to help people in meaningful, life-affirming ways. It was the best decision I've ever made. My only wish is that I'd done it sooner.

Now is the right time for you to be and do what you've always wanted. Imagine getting out of bed each day with newfound energy because you're living your authentic life. You can almost feel the underlying hum of positivity that will carry you through, knowing you're spending your time the way you want to, and sharing your greatness with the people who deserve you most.

Nothing is as personally powerful as summoning your

strength to make changes and then doing the hard work to get there. Once you do, you can eliminate the phrase "I wish I would have" from your vocabulary and celebrate your ability to take on rewarding challenges in your life, and win.

PREPARE AND PLAN FOR CHANGE WITH A PROCESS

This manual will guide you through a three-part transformation process and lead you to bravely make the changes you desire. You'll find easy-to-digest steps that break down activities for you to quickly learn and use. Key themes will be emphasized at the end of the chapters, and there will be opportunities to self-reflect and work on a better you.

Part One, "Inspiration," gives an overview of the process and highlights the impact of inspirational stories. Sharing my story helps to emphasize how vital the mind shifts and methods you'll learn are for making your changes. The lessons adopted along the way are the backbone of the rest of the book, and this will be a motivational read for you.

Part Two, "Preparation," teaches a myriad of mental, physical, and spiritual approaches to get you ready. This section is chock-full of tools for you to use, and each chapter builds on the previous ones. Messages about loving, trusting, and being comfortable with yourself are interspersed with exercises and practices that support your healthy body and mind, and will help you more openly relate to the people around you.

Part Three, "Your Plan for Change," is about getting down to business and doing the work of your transformation. You'll discover ways to get unstuck and get clear on the details of what, why, and how to change. Holding yourself accountable to your specific goals is the secret sauce in your success, so you'll create and work your plan to encourage that success and stay motivated until you've done what you set out to do.

We are meant to live purposeful lives with strong, connected personal relationships and fulfilling careers. I called upon my strength to make significant changes after 40 and wrote this book to help other women. I am here to empower you to work through your sticking points and gain the courage and skills to transition yourself into a happier life.

My new path as a life coach has allowed me to work closely with a group of remarkable women. I've created this process, with its practices and accountability methods, based on their needs for change. I've watched their self-esteem grow as they've brought passion and these pivotal habits into their lives to help them reach their goals and thrive.

This book is about finding the right way ahead for you, regardless of what the people closest to you, society, and even that scared voice in your head tell you. It's not *just* a feel-good rah-rah story with an "I did it and you can do it, too" attitude. If you put in the hard work and incorporate what you learn here into your life, you will find fulfillment.

Don't wait for the proverbial truck to come along and force you into action. Understand that you have the power to transform your own life. Consider this your starting point. Trust that even a small desire to make a change can move you into great things and open your mind to new possibilities.

PART ONE

INSPIRATION

"Life's not about expecting, hoping and wishing,
it's about doing, being and becoming."

—MIKE DOOLEY

CHAPTER ONE

THE THREE-PART TRANSFORMATION PROCESS FOR CHANGE

I learned to cook late in life and found that the secret to my success is following the recipe to the letter. There is something comforting about the process, with a defined beginning, middle, and end, and guidance for the steps in between. I find cooking becomes more enjoyable and less anxiety-provoking when there are clear directions to follow. I've come to appreciate a detailed, well-thought-out plan, and recognized the same need in the women around me who are seeking change.

This chapter is an overview of the journey you're about to begin. We'll review the list of approaches and practices you'll be folding into your life, and you'll learn the best way to use this quick and easy-to-use manual for maximum effect. Know that you have the strength for change; you only need inspiration and a clearly defined method to empower, prepare, and teach you how to construct the plan that will lead you there.

VISUALIZE THE THREE-PART PROCESS

The number three holds power. It's the smallest number that creates a pattern, there's a rhythm to using it, and your mind is more likely to remember information presented in threes. It's a symbol of luck in some cultures, and three is often referred to as the number for optimism. It can also signify communication, connection, and creativity.

As you read this book, you'll find this number (or multiples of it), in many lists, references, and practices. To this end, imagine the three-part process as a massive stairway, with six wider and taller steps at the base; mid-way up, there is a large landing followed by three final stairs that will take you to the top. In Part One (Inspiration), you'll find yourself staring up at the ambitious climb before you. This section is designed to help you gather your courage and begin your ascent.

The six thicker steps near the bottom represent Part Two. Each chapter in this section provides preparation and the foundation you need for your transformation. These six steps are tall (too tall to skip any in between), and each stair relies on its inherent strength and your ability to scale the previous one.

Once you've completed this second part of the process, you'll be better conditioned to take on the final stretch. You'll also have a group of people waiting for you on the landing to support and cheer you on as you take the final three stairs. Each chapter in Part Three will help you create your plan and set you up for success to take your last steps and carry out your change.

9 STEPS TO CHANGE AND FULFILLMENT

Here are the key lessons and activities by step as you're climbing your staircase of change:

PART ONE: INSPIRATION
(standing at the bottom of the stairs)

- Be inspired to action with an inspirational story of struggle and change.

PART TWO: PREPARATION
(climbing the foundational six steps, reaching the landing)

- Step 1: Start with self-love and a writing practice for use with this book and beyond.

- Step 2: Create a strong base with a healthy space, good habits, and gratitude.
- Step 3: Embrace positivity and use the Law of Attraction to draw what you want to you.
- Step 4: Learn the life-changing practices of mindfulness and meditation.
- Step 5: Find and use your inner voice and distinguish it from your ego.
- Step 6: Gather a support network and get comfortable with yourself.

PART THREE: YOUR PLAN FOR CHANGE
(the final ascent—taking your final three steps)

- Step 7: Get unstuck, get clear about your change, and overcome impostor syndrome.
- Step 8: Create SMART goals and your plan for change.
- Step 9: Finish strong with a daily plan, share your progress, and project success.

HOW THIS BOOK WORKS BEST

The order of the chapters is purposeful, so the book should be read in order and new concepts assimilated in sequence. Chapters build on what you've learned along the way, and each step will lead you to your jumping-off point, where you will have the readiness and assuredness to make changes. You can always go back and review the chapters separately to brush up on their teachings, but the process will be most effective if you read the lessons in order.

You'll find a section at the end of most chapters titled "Wrap It Up" that highlights the most important points. There's work for you to do in Parts Two and Three, and the section "Do the Work" will encourage you to contemplate questions and take actions that tie into the themes from that step. The more you engage with the thinking, writing, and implementation of what you read, especially if these ideas are new to you, the sooner they'll become a part of you.

IF YOUR FIRST RESPONSE IS NO

Everyone's journey is different. The choices I made will be different than those you will make, and that's how it should be. Your idea of happiness is uniquely yours and should be celebrated accordingly. Along those lines, the combination of tools you choose to inspire and energize yourself may be different than those selected by other women, but the more of these practices you can knit into your being, the more adaptable you'll be to change.

As you look through the chapters, you may come across concepts that are foreign to you, like the Law of Attraction, or raising your vibrational energy. You may even have an initial reaction that says, "This is not for me." We often push back on things that are new as an automatic, internal protective measure that we can't control (hello, ego), and we'll touch on this topic again.

If you find yourself in this situation, read the chapter and revisit the ideas to see if they resonate. Change involves creating new mindsets and habits. You may be pleasantly surprised at how easily you can integrate one of these fresh ideas, or even how necessary one is to your ability to take big steps forward.

PART INSPIRATION AND PART INFORMATION

I'm a combination of gut feeling, empirical evidence, and belief all wrapped together. It's an interesting mix of science and spirituality that works for me. At first, I had to hide my witchy intuition and touchy-feely feelings in the business world, but those gut feelings, combined with my love of process and overarching desire to just get things done, served me well and led me here.

This book follows the way my mind works. It's partly inspirational and partly informational because you'll be best served by using the different parts of you, like your inner voice and brain, to make decisions that will shape your life moving forward. If this isn't something you're already doing, you'll be able to do so by the time you're finished!

Where science or reason can help you better understand what

you're reading, I've included it. My curious mind likes to know the how and why of things, but I've kept it simple so you don't get caught up in the minutia. Knowing the background of a skill or approach may give you more confidence in its efficacy and make you even more inclined to add it to your life.

COMMIT THREE WEEKS TO THE TOOLS OF PREPARATION

The preparation in Part Two can dramatically improve your outlook. Even if your goal for change is not health-based, you'll benefit from building a healthy base to create the best version of you, and the other lessons will serve you in your everyday life. By using these practices as part of this specific process, you'll be invigorated and more motivated to try new things, and even more likely to succeed.

Commit to using what you learn in "Preparation" for three straight weeks. Dedicating a full month may mentally be too long, and two weeks is just not long enough to allow these great actions to take root in your life. You can continue reading and start building your plan during this time, but make the effort to turn these tools into habits through 21 days of consistent use.

WRAP IT UP

Making your change should not feel like a blind leap of

faith off a cliff. Rather, with the orderly process and step-by-step instructions included in this book, you'll learn the ground-up mechanics to stair-step your way through your transformation and become an even higher version of yourself. Follow the flow of the chapters and commit yourself to your preparation to get the most out of your work.

Consider this chapter the list of ingredients and techniques you'll use in your own recipe for change. With these in hand, ready yourself to be inspired to make your own life better. Inspiration compels you to act and plays an important role in believing you can attain your goals, so we'll use it as our starting point for Chapters Two and Three.

CHAPTER TWO

WHAT WE WANT AND NEED MATTERS

Beneath it all, I'm just a girl from the South Side of Chicago who made difficult decisions regarding relationships, the right way to raise my son, and my career, in order to live the life that was meant for me. My huge capacity for love and care compelled me to share my pain and this process with women like you, looking to overcome their own challenges and limiting beliefs so they can make changes and live the life they want.

Each part of this book holds lessons learned in response to what I wanted and needed in my own life. I'm sharing my story in support of you, to inspire you to create your own, and to demonstrate the profound influence the things you'll learn here can have on your life. We'll start this chapter by emphasizing the importance of inspirational stories, move through my story of struggle, and into my story of change in Chapter Three.

HOW INSPIRATIONAL STORIES HELP

Inspiration can lift our mind, emotions, and body, which then elevates our feelings and activity level, and gives us an overall sense of wellness and happiness. Inspiration opens us up to new possibilities by exposing us to extraordinary experiences, helping us to visualize moving beyond our limitations. When inspired, we are more likely to give new approaches or practices a go, have a stronger desire to excel in them, and have a higher sense of self-esteem and belief in our own abilities.

Stories help create connections between people and ideas. They build trust and allow us to be more open to learning. They're also impactful for all three types of learners, and whether you're a visual learner (learning best by seeing and reading), an auditory learner (learning best by hearing and discussing), or a kinesthetic learner (learning best by doing, experiencing, or feeling), hearing a story will resonate and stick with you. Important facts or lessons are much more likely to be remembered if they're part of a story.

Through inspirational stories, we look for role models that have similar life experiences or challenges and seek inspiration from their efforts. We are more likely to act and put in hard work of our own if we read or hear stories of other people we can relate to, who are rewarded for their hard work by attaining their goals. When inspired, we set inspired (and loftier) goals, which help push us to make further reaching changes.

START WITH A STORY OF STRUGGLE

I was painfully shy in social situations in my pre-teen years, something that still shows up on occasion, but now I can breathe my way through it. I had a secret daily struggle with self-esteem no one else saw, and I didn't realize until I was much older that I also had anxiety. Bathrooms became safe places for me to hide when I was overwhelmed, or when being around a bunch of people was too much for me.

My parents put me in gymnastics when I was 6 because I was hyperactive (Mom's words), and I stuck with it until I was 14. Having practice every day kept me from normal kid stuff like going to middle school basketball games, and because of my shyness, it was just plain hard for me to make friends. Not surprisingly, I was bullied in seventh and eighth grade by a group of mean girls who would push me down, or knock my books out of my hands and say horrific things to me.

I forgave them, and the ones with good hearts became my friends in high school; in fact, some even became my earliest coaching projects. I helped them push themselves outside of their comfort zones and try new things. I encouraged them to pursue what they wanted even if it felt like a huge risk, and most of the time they got what they went after.

DECIDE TO MAKE IT DIFFERENT

I made the decision that things were going to be different on the first day of high school. *I* was going to be different. I chose to be happier and more outgoing, and it gave me my first glimpse of the potential of positivity and the power it held for me.

With a new confidence, I discovered cheerleading my freshman year, and it set me up to be a supporter of people for the rest of my life. Gymnastics had made me strong, so I was usually the person on the bottom pushing everyone else up or I was catching them on their way down in pyramids and stunts. My mom said I'd had an innate ability to find the people who either needed to be pushed up or caught from the time I was in preschool.

After four good years of high school, I was mentally ready for a big school and was accepted to the University of Illinois at Urbana-Champaign. I pushed myself to take full advantage of what college had to offer, and I absolutely got it. I majored in microbiology, was part of the marching band as a member of the Illinettes Dance Team, and started bartending at the tender age of 19, which, honestly, might have been the most useful part of my education.

I'd worked hard in high school and college, keeping my anxiety at bay and my optimism high, and accomplished almost anything I put my mind to. My parents worried about how I would handle major disappointment, because I never seemed to come face to face with it when I was younger. I had no idea then, but that part was still to come.

OUR NEED FOR SUPPORT IS REAL

I graduated from college and came back home to live, having absolutely no idea what to do next. By chance, I walked into a nightclub on Fulton Street in Chicago and asked if they needed any help. I was hired on the spot and started working there that night at the age of 21.

Bartending there was the closest I'd ever come to being a rock star, and it was the perfect thing for me to do in my early to mid-twenties. We hosted one of the biggest parties in the city each weekend and laughed like idiots as we counted our tips at the end of the night. We served celebrities and athletes on a regular basis, but also had our fair share of everyday jerks to contend with.

Being hired that day was a momentous event in my life. I found a group of smart and stunning women that I count among my closest friends, along with some of the most caring and protective men I've ever met. I was also introduced to my former husband there.

There's a kinship we all share, having worked so closely together at that time in our lives. I was hard-pressed to make the same type of loyal friendships as I moved through my next twenty years, and losing touch with this group of supporters was a major misstep for me.

"Sometimes the old ways are the best."

—NAOMIE HARRIS AS EVE IN *SKYFALL*

Working at night allowed me to spend my days with my grandmother, one of the toughest and coolest chicks I've ever known. She grew up during the Depression, had six kids and raised them in a one-bedroom apartment in the house her father had built, and buried one of her children and husband in less than two years' time. My grandmother is one of my strongest role models, and I'm incredibly lucky to have had that time with her.

She wasn't afraid of anyone or anything and was unapologetically herself; I greatly admire her for that. I have an interesting traditional streak that runs through me, relating to men's and women's roles in relationships, and it may very well have been the time I spent with my grandmother that helped reinforce these old-timey notions in me. I was able to temporarily squash them, but they came to bear the first day I went back to work after having my son, and just about every day after that for 14 years.

"Nobody ever tells you don't get married, don't buy a house, and don't have children."

—MY FATHER

While everything else was going well, I struggled in my relationships with men throughout college and into my twenties.

I felt like no one really understood me and I couldn't trust anyone with my easily broken heart. I had built up a hard candy shell exterior, but was still a 12-year-old girl on the inside. Trusting men, and more importantly letting them in, was an ongoing challenge.

I talked with my parents about the fact that marriage might not be for me. My father threw a monkey wrench into my plans and told me he wanted a grandson, so I put tying the knot on my to-do list. The pressures of juggling a full-blown career, being married, and having a son were about to damn near destroy me, but I thought I could, and above all, that I was *supposed to*, have and do it all.

CAREFUL WHAT YOU WISH FOR

There often comes a time in a hospitality worker's life when they just can't stand serving customers anymore. Even ridiculous amounts of money can't keep you from secretly wanting to jump over the bar and go after rude people. Everyone's social skills can benefit from spending time in the service industry, but I knew it was time for me to move on. I was ready to use my other skills.

September 11, 2001, should have been my first day on the distribution side of the wine industry. I left the house that morning to get my car washed and came back to see the second plane slam into the World Trade Center on the TV. If

I were more in tune with the universe at that point, I might have seen this (happening on the first day of a new job) as a sign of what was to come for me in the following years. I wasn't ready to see the signs, and I plowed ahead with the exuberance of youth.

I quickly moved through the early stages of my wine career, having found the right champion in my District Manager. She was a powerhouse of a woman with a wicked sense of humor, and she helped me grind through the first few years as I dragged a bag of samples around town, hating every minute of being a wine salesperson. (Hate is not a word I use lightly. It's reserved for things that I truly despise, like Chicago winters.)

I'd gone from sitting in on friendly and lively wine sales calls as a restaurant manager to becoming a salesperson, hearing "no" on a daily basis, and having to scramble when people canceled at the last minute or didn't show up. There was no way to set and keep a schedule. It was a good lesson about the things I didn't want in a job, so I began to focus on what I *did* want, and imagined what that job might feel like.

Coincidentally (actually synchronistically, but more on that later), a marketing position with regular office hours and less everyday rejection opened up, and I was given the opportunity to take it on. I loved it. Shortly after, our little company was bought by a larger behemoth, and as soon as

I finished watching the welcome video that featured older men in suits at the table and women serving the coffee, I knew I needed to go.

I found the right fit in a family-owned fine wine company, built on a culture of excellence. I loved the attention to detail that was paid to every aspect of the business and the fast pace of it, and I learned an incredible amount in a short time. It was like drinking from a fire hose, and my mind was happy with the challenge of it.

I was pregnant within a year of being hired and wasn't sure how the news would be received. In what was then an even more male-dominated industry, I was one of only a handful of women in the company and the first one to have a baby. I was thrilled and terrified at once when I was told I would be coming back to work after maternity leave with a promotion to Vice President, General Manager.

ADD MOTHERHOOD TO THE MIX

The birth of my son was the most important moment of my life. Like most mothers, words can't describe the depth of love and adoration I have for him. I took three months off from work with him, and it was not enough.

I didn't want to schlep him in and out of the house for his first year, so we hired a young, energetic nanny with a

Montessori background. Her need for cleanliness and order were a godsend, and I felt pretty good about handing my little peanut over to her. We could hardly afford her, and I could barely get out the door the first day. Although being home with him in the very beginning was tough, not being home with him was worse for me.

At that point, people would say I had two children: my son and the company. I was leaving the house early, working long hours, and then picking him up the minute I walked in the door and not putting him down until I laid him in bed. The concept of work-life balance was years away and the company needed me, so I muscled my way through it.

I felt that my presence and the energy I brought to each workday helped moved the company forward. I was constantly moving through the office at breakneck speed, recharging my batteries with movement and nearly running people over because there was so much to do. It was hard not to be a workaholic. There were issues brewing in my married life, so it was easier to dive into work rather than meet them head-on.

TO HELL IN A HANDBASKET

The mind-numbing exhaustion and stress coming from both work and home left me with such a feeling of unhappiness that I decided to go to therapy when my son was a year old.

I saw the therapist my friends were seeing, and he came highly recommended. The whole thing felt selfish to me back then, but it shouldn't have. In my mind, I was already away from my son entirely too much, and now I was taking two additional hours each week to fight traffic, get down to the city, overpay for parking, and then talk about myself.

In addition to the overwhelm I was already feeling, I was on the cusp of a character-building ten-year period that started with my mother's breast cancer, followed by my father's motorcycle accident, and finished with the lung cancer diagnosis and sudden death of the president of our company. I wasn't listening to my inner voice at that point as it urged me to slow down—I just couldn't. I was wired to take care of everyone else and put their needs first; I thought I could shove everything down and it would all be fine.

Social media started around this same time and I wanted no part of it. I'm a very private person as it is, but I started to feel like such a complete and total failure because I couldn't put myself out there. I didn't have the desire to be open with anyone for fear they would see what a mess I was on the inside. I set up an account and put up a picture of 6-year-old me in my Brownie uniform. It was just easier.

It looked like the rest of the women in the working world could have it all and do it all, but I could not. After feeling like I could take on anything for so many years, I felt like I couldn't hack it anymore, and it seemed like I was failing at absolutely everything. I watched my friends connect with each other and knew I was emotionally slipping away. I was hiding from them in plain sight but couldn't do it forever.

EVER WISH YOU GOT HIT BY A TRUCK?

I was running myself ragged and getting sick on such a regular basis it was scary. I entertained thoughts of some sort of minor catastrophe on my drive into work, like getting hit by a truck to get me off the treadmill I was on. I thought I would be diagnosed with a horrific disease, but my doctor told me it was just stress.

I laughed at it all because I thought I was supposed to be Superwoman, and Superwoman doesn't get stressed. She can have a career and a family, do it all on little sleep, wear nice outfits, and smile all the time. I did eventually end up in the emergency room with chest pains and what turned out to be a full-blown panic attack.

That trip to the hospital was the warning sign that I finally heeded. My body and spirit simply started breaking down because I had ignored my needs for so long. It was time for me to make changes and not stay stuck in a life that was no longer serving me.

SMALL CHANGES CREATE ENERGY
FOR LARGER ONES

Eleven years after joining the company that had come to define me, it was sold and integrated into a larger organization. The sale had been an arduous process, and it did nothing to help my family life. Regardless, I made a commitment to stay on to ensure that the ideals, principles, and care of the relationships we had worked so hard to create would remain intact.

I took a work trip to Argentina shortly after the purchase was complete. I used it to expand my own horizons after so many years of being dutiful to everything and everyone else around me. It was revitalizing to spend time with people from all over the world, and I can remember looking at myself in the mirror one morning and thinking, "I remember you." It was the exact spark I needed, and that shift in my scenery set off a chain of events that eventually led to the right way ahead for me.

I got a surge of energy from the trip that was followed by a flurry of activity when I got back, and even earned the nickname "Get Shit Done Girl" from my boss. I dug into my work. I was creating and executing plans at a high level, inspiring the people around me, and my confidence in myself and my abilities was growing.

Soon after, I began to recognize my gifts and understand

my knack for making people feel comfortable and allowing them to be vulnerable. I started having conversations with our suppliers and employees that had more to do with their personal lives than the business at hand. My office became the site of closed-door meetings where people came in and let their guard down, and I would listen and guide them as best I could.

I loved those talks and they fulfilled me. They allowed me to consider my wants and needs, and were my first inkling that I didn't need to have or do it all if it didn't make me happy. I was beginning to understand that my authentic life was waiting for me, and I just needed to find the strength and tools to make changes that would let me live as my true self.

CHAPTER THREE

FINISH WITH A STORY OF CHANGE

After discovering my gift for helping others, it was time for me to help myself. I knew the responsibility for making changes resided in me, and I drew upon my resolve to find the ways to do it.

MEDITATION VS. MEDICATION

My son's father and I ended up in couples' therapy to try and save our marriage, but it was already too late. Our therapist could see how different we were; we had grown too far apart, and she noted how frazzled I was. She suggested I consider taking an antidepressant, and I told her I wanted to try meditation first. It was an offhand comment, but I had just read about meditation and figured I would give it a try.

She was hugely supportive, and I began meditating first

thing in the morning after I had my coffee, while the house was still quiet. It helped me silence the voice in my head that told me I was a fake, or that I was failing, or anything else that would bounce around in there and keep me from being in the moment. I gained a sense of peace and calm that I'd never had before, and using that morning time for myself was my first formal act of self-love on my journey of change.

Shortly after making meditation part of my daily routine, I took my first trip alone to a wellness resort with a soul-soothing spa at the foot of the mountains in Arizona. (I chose Miraval for many reasons, and the fact they served wine in the evenings was admittedly among them.) I couldn't remember the last time I did something of that magnitude entirely for me. The trip gave me the opportunity to completely break down, build myself back up, and prepare for divorce.

It was there that I started journaling and wrote a love letter to myself, experienced the intensity of group meditation, and learned how to practice mindfulness. I sat in the same overstuffed chaise lounge for six hours straight one day, watching the sun shift and set over the mountains. I summoned my inner strength on that trip and gained a deep understanding of the power I possessed. I immediately called upon it when I returned home and began to make changes.

MOVE ON WITH RESPECT AND RISE

I went through one of the most amicable divorces possible at the age of 41. I chose to honor my former husband as my son's father, and it informed my entire approach. I don't refer to him as my ex; he will forever be a part of both my past and my future, and the word "former" has a kinder, more positive connotation.

I worked to keep animosity and blame out of the process and made smart decisions with my son's happiness in mind. After trying to stick it out because I couldn't bear the thought of not seeing him every single day, it reached the point where it made more sense for my son to have two houses filled with love, rather than one full of anger and bitterness. It was one of the most unselfish and painful decisions I've ever made, and I still choke back tears on occasion when he leaves to spend days at his father's house.

As much as I knew my marriage could not have continued, I mourned the loss of the life I thought I should have had. I wrapped my arms around the emotions and decided to feel it all, to move with it and through it rather than avoid it, but I would not let the negativity or the sadness take hold of me. I worked to shift my thoughts away from despair to see the possibilities in each new day and appreciate the positivity my actions had brought for me and my son.

Eventually, there was relief, and the daily underlying tension and grind of resentment was gone. Music became the back-drop of my life and kept my energy high, and meditation and early morning runs through the neighborhood became habit. I recovered and reconnected in real ways with my close circle of friends, and I was happy to have their support.

It was during this time I decided to teach myself how to cook. Good, healthy food, green juice, and clean living were medicine for my body and soul and the source of my strength. People took notice of the changes in me and said I looked healthier than I had in years.

I didn't have a big blowout divorce party or start hanging out in bars again looking for a good time. I'd had enough of that in my twenties and was content to work in my garden and spend the alone time healing. I was busy building the base of health I needed for my next feat of change.

PUT YOUR OXYGEN MASK ON FIRST

After two years of being single, I allowed myself to visualize the man I wanted by my side. He would be fun and kind-hearted, and he would *get* me. At the age of 43, I willed him into being and drew him into my life by unknowingly cracking his computer screen on a flight to California for a work trip.

He's one of the most patient men I've ever met, because

dating after divorce with a child is challenging. Working mother guilt and not having my son with me every day made my time with him that much more precious, especially during the middle school years. My boyfriend was left out many times as I needed to build a stronger relationship with my son.

My boyfriend takes care of me when I let him, and I find that I'm doing that more often. It's taken a long time, but I'm slowly shedding the idea that I need to do absolutely everything on my own. He has also taught me the importance of being good to myself, to put my oxygen mask on first, and not put everyone else's needs before mine.

As it turns out, I'm really not that difficult to understand. Yes, I'm stubborn and emotional. I'm a ball of energy punctuated by 20-minute naps in the summer, and a homebody that hibernates in the winter. At the end of it all, he tells me the three most important words anyone has ever said, "I know you."

"YOU DON'T BELONG HERE."

One of my coworkers dropped this line on me out of the blue a few years after the sale of our wine company, when it had been fully absorbed. I was beginning to believe that truer words were never spoken. I didn't belong there, and I knew in my heart there was something greater for me to do in the service of others. I just wasn't quite ready to leave behind a well-paying job, the security that comes with it, or the people I had worked with for almost 20 years.

And, at 45 years old, I was afraid. I didn't know if I could weather another life-altering change.

Promises that were made when the company was sold had been broken, and the atmosphere was becoming aggressive and corporate. My plan was to stick it out, suck it up, and stay until I was 50, but it became increasingly difficult. I watched the personality drain out of my coworkers, and the early passing of a dear friend and colleague made me realize how fragile life could be. In addition, my son needed me more than ever, and I wanted to connect with him on a deeper level after so many tumultuous years.

While everyone else was leaning in, I was looking for the exit to get out. It was time for me to find myself and become the real me. It was time to stop sitting in meetings where I didn't care about what was being said, with half the room not paying attention and most of what was discussed falling short of being accomplished. I was seeking inspiration and connection and a way to help people. I didn't know where I was going to find them, but I was ready to figure it out.

Everyone wanted to know why, as one of a small group of

female executives in the industry at that time, I was leaving. I told them I had climbed the corporate ladder, rang the bell, and was climbing back down to find what was next for me. It was not a popular move with the women who saw me as an inspirational female figure, but it was the right one for me. I had gotten so far away from who I truly was on the inside that I felt like I was living someone else's life.

I finally left my job and career behind when my son graduated from eighth grade. I had no specific idea about what I'd do next, but I promised myself I would take three full months to decompress, get my house in order, and not think about it. Thoughts about what I might do would bubble up, but I left them in the back of my mind to simmer and have the chance to fully form.

I had time to do things I hadn't done in years. I got a pool pass, tore through three easy-reading novels, and spent the summer being there for my son when he needed me. We bought his first football cleats together, I took him to his first football practice, and I embraced any opportunity for us to hang together because I was making up for lost mom time with him.

There is a significant loss of self that happens when you leave a job, especially one where you've worked with the same people for a long time. As fall gave way to winter, I began to miss the comfort of my previous job. When you've put on a suit of armor (which was a sheath dress and heels for me) and pretended to be someone or something else for so long, you grieve, even though you're in a better place. It's just part of the process.

BECAUSE YOU CAN DOESN'T MEAN YOU SHOULD

I started the official search for my next career, working at least six hours a day to do research and put together a plan. I read for weeks about the best career changes if you want to help people, took tests, and tried to avoid the articles that said how hard it is to change your career if you're over 40. It was surprising to see all the doubters out there, and I chose to ignore them.

I explored the idea of being a social worker because it kept coming up on those "best" lists. I would need to go back to school for two years to get a master's degree, pay an enormous amount of money, and then go through years of training before I'd be licensed and able to directly help people. It was an expensive proposition, and a challenging one, but I felt like having an advanced degree would confirm that I was smart, and my career as an executive had not somehow been a fluke.

Impostor syndrome was not yet on my radar, so thankfully my inner voice objected to the plan, and then the universe sounded the alarm. I wrote my admissions paper, pulled together my transcripts and was granted an interview, but something wasn't sitting right with me. I went back and forth about the cost and time commitment and ended up openly consulting the universe on whether or not this was the right road for me to take.

I said out loud, "If this is what I'm supposed to do, show me a sign." I got my answer. Within days I was rear-ended on the highway, not too far from the site of that interview.

I declined the offer to join the program. I decided the universe had indeed spoken with a firm "NO" and the accident was a warning against the wreck I would've made of my time with my son and my finances. This road was not for me, but it had given me a shot of confidence and the opportunity to write extensively for the first time in years. I felt like I was ready to take the right path when I found it.

WHERE ATTENTION GOES, ENERGY FLOWS

I channeled my energy and invested my time in making myself the best version I could be. I bought a used rowing machine to hop on first thing in the morning after meditation and grabbed a few minutes of mindfulness as often as I could to keep me present and inspire my intuition. I filled my days with gratitude for my might and the decisions I had made, and I felt like I was on the verge of my next step when something clicked.

Life coaching had come up on my radar multiple times as I researched my next career path, and I decided to take a course. I knew this was the start of my next great adventure just a few weeks into the class. I had been coaching everyone around me for so long, but hadn't fully realized it. It was as if someone had lit a fire inside of me.

It took four weeks to write copy, put together a website, and get up and running on social media. I'd never experienced such a period of blazing creativity and optimism. I'm an up-with-the-sun kind of girl, and when I'm moving in the right direction, I have boundless energy. It felt like I was 35 again, not 47.

I'd wake up early and get on my computer to write, and the words just poured out of me. I wrote the most nakedly honest things about myself and put it out there for everyone to see and encouraged other women to take great chances on making changes. I'd taken the largest steps ever to be open and connected with the good people around me, and this was such an incredible process of renewal and rediscovery.

I'm now working with a varied group of loving and giving women, who need support to find their strength and a plan for their change. Some have gone through divorce and have children, and some never married and took other paths. Regardless of their journey, I firmly believe I've been put on this planet to help women be fearless in the face of change.

I'm more myself now than I've ever been, and it's exhilarating. I am grateful for having had so many strong and empowering female role models in my life; I want my story to inspire as many women as humanly possible to find their way to their own personal happiness. I've forgiven myself for being human and for not being perfect, and I'm here to help other women do the same.

Begin to imagine where you'll finish your story of change. You don't need to know exactly how to get there, only where you want to go. Now, let's get you ready.

PART TWO

PREPARATION

"Your life does not get better by chance, it gets better by change."

—JIM ROHN

CHAPTER FOUR

STEP 1: A LITTLE SELF-LOVE GOES A LONG WAY

Your story of change begins where mine ended, with the most important support of all: self-love. The ease with which you'll move through your transformation depends on the care you give yourself and your understanding of what is necessary to be at your best. Responding to your own needs may be foreign to you, but it helps you create a nurturing internal environment that allows you to accept and adore every piece of you, even the things you consider to be flaws or weaknesses.

We want to be loved for exactly who we are, and it starts within *us*. Love yourself and hold yourself to a high standard for your own happiness as you look to make changes. Now is the time to take your first step. Here, we'll reflect on self-love and activities that promote it, have you write a letter to yourself to get the love flowing, then delve into journaling, including its benefits and how to get started.

WHAT IS SELF-LOVE?

Self-love is an appreciation of yourself and regard for your own physical, psychological, and spiritual well-being. It grows from the actions you take in being good to yourself and showing yourself compassion, the way you would with one of your oldest and dearest friends. Don't think for a minute that practicing self-love is being selfish in any way.

To use self-love as it relates to your desire for change, make peace with who you've been in the past and who you are now. Give a nod to what you've been through, understand how it shaped you, and then let it go. Your work here is forward-looking and forward-thinking.

Forgiving yourself for being human and for not being perfect is one of the greatest expressions of self-love. We'll revisit the theme of perfection, but the sooner you realize no one is perfect, including you, the kinder and gentler you will be with yourself. You'll also be less hesitant and more willing to try new things and more likely to change up your everyday routine.

6 ACTIVITIES THAT PROMOTE SELF-LOVE:

1. Practice self-care by nourishing your body with what it needs to be healthy. We'll dive into the details in the next chapter.

2. Be compassionate with yourself on days when you don't feel your best or most confident, so you can heal and bounce back. Know that it's a temporary state and beating yourself up about it will only delay your recovery.

3. Treat yourself with personal experiences. Spend quality alone time by doing special things by yourself, like having a cup of coffee solo with a piece of cake at your favorite café, or getting a massage.

4. Write a love letter to yourself. Be your own admirer and rejoice in the magnificence that is you. Once you've finished, you can mail it to yourself and read it for full effect when it arrives.

5. Journal. You can write out all the good and bad thoughts and feelings you have about yourself so the negative ones don't fester, and the positive ones gain strength.

6. Honor yourself by saying "no" to things you don't want to do. Be selective about how you spend your time and who you spend it with. Saying "yes" and being half-heartedly engaged will only drag you down, especially if it's with people who don't lift you up.

SELF-LOVE AND SETTING BOUNDARIES

Putting self-love into practice may be unfamiliar territory for you. If so, start by believing you're deserving of your love, add activities to your day that foster self-love, and begin to pay attention to what makes you feel uncomfortable or stressed. Set boundaries when you feel this way to ensure you can do more of the things that are important to you, that you enjoy.

Having healthy guidelines, rules, or limits will increase your self-esteem and empower you to say yes (and no!) to others and mean it. When you feel the need to set a boundary with someone, do it in a clear, calm, and resolute way. Communicate with love and respect, and understand you are not responsible for the response you get.

If you're new to speaking up about your needs, you may feel anxious, guilty, or even angry, and use too many words to overexplain your point. If this happens, focus and remember that this is a worthwhile demonstration of your self-respect. Working through these feelings may take some getting used to, but like any other skill, confidently and assertively setting your boundaries will become easier the more you do it.

As your self-love grows, especially if you tend to put other people's needs before your own, you may find yourself saying "no" to social invitations more frequently. Be firm with yourself and those around you, graciously but without apology, and have conviction in communicating your message. If you're dying for a soak in the tub or a few hours alone in your pajamas to rest and recharge, the people who truly love and support you will understand when you tell them you can't be with them.

WRITE A LOVE LETTER TO YOURSELF

Let's get things rolling by having you write a love letter to yourself. It's a wonderful way to be reminded why you deserve to have what you want in life, and that you've got the grit to get it. Keep it in a convenient place, refer to it often, and call upon it when you need it most. This is a personal testament of your own greatness, to be used when you need encouragement or to help you summon your strength throughout this process.

I carried a wine bag and had a sales route early in my career. Rejection is part of the day-to-day of a salesperson, and sometimes the customers just don't want what you're selling. Most of the time it rolls off your back and you move on to the next account.

On especially hard days, when every answer was "no" and my confidence was in the dumps, I went to the restaurants or shops where I had great relationships. I knew the managers and employees would be happy just to see me walk through the door. It was the ultimate pick-me-up to help me finish those days with my head held high.

Your love letter to yourself can be used in the same way. On your difficult days you can read your letter and remember exactly why you're worthy and up to the challenge of making changes. You can celebrate the strong and stunning parts of you and get yourself back on track.

Answer these questions and take the time to fully consider and write out your responses:

- What are the things you really love and admire about yourself?
- What traits do you feel define you?
- What parts of you and your personality are you most proud of?
- What are the things other people consistently compliment or say about you? (Know that you may not always hear these as loudly and clearly as you should.)
- What are you grateful for in yourself? Get specific and list as many things as come to mind.
- What are you grateful for in your life?

YOU CAN'T CHANGE EVERYTHING AT ONCE

Once you've finished your personal love fest, it's time to move on to the reason why you're reading this book. What do you need to change to live the life you want? Write down every single change you feel would be truly impactful.

Spend time with the list. Let it seep in. You'll eventually want to pick the most important thing to focus on first, because you can't change everything at once.

You need your energy and determination to be laser-focused, not scatter-shot by trying to change too many things at the same time. The remaining steps in this section hone in on your preparation, so you don't need to definitively decide today what to change first (though you probably already know what it is).

JOURNALING

Journaling is the regular recording of your thoughts, feelings, and ideas to help you more easily understand them. It's a place for you to openly convey your positive and negative emotions so you can gain an understanding of what makes you happy and what you want in your life. It can also help you discover what is upsetting to you and what you should avoid or adjust. In the context of this book, journaling can be a tremendous tool for discovery.

You can write on a legal pad or in a special notebook or journal, type on a computer, or record in any other way you feel you can best express yourself. Choose the setup that gets you writing to unlock your innermost thoughts and lets you get them all out so you can learn from them and move on. The trick here is to keep the method you choose nearby so you can write when you are inspired to do so.

That said, there's an intimacy and neural connection formed when you use pen or pencil on paper to write instead of typing, and this will serve you later in this book when you begin to formally create your goals and plan. Typing out your journal entries can be training wheels to help you connect with and communicate your feelings and needs, especially if this is your usual way to capture thoughts and send information. If you're interested, get comfortable with your mental process around journaling as you type, then eventually change the physical process and try handwriting.

Write, type, sketch, or even doodle; do whatever you want in the way you need to do it. This is a no judgment zone, and no one else will ever see what you've written unless you want them to. Be kind and don't criticize yourself for anything you say here, or how you say it.

HOW JOURNALING HELPS

Journaling has been shown to improve memory and communication skills and help you get better sleep, which can lead to a stronger immune system, increase your self-confidence, and aid in getting over the pain of trauma or loss more quickly. By way of journaling, you can be your own therapist. You get to say whatever you want, however you want, whenever you want. As an added bonus, it doesn't come with a hefty price tag or expensive parking.

People often have multiple problems or issues swirl around in their head at the same time. Journaling forces you to focus on a single thing and may help you work through challenges and find solutions for yourself. You also can become your own personal pep squad and write uplifting, optimistic views on who you are and what your bright future looks like.

Having the ability to formally document your thoughts and feelings gives you the opportunity to review your writing and recognize your growth. A large part of making successful changes is seeing and celebrating your progression. Looking back on where you were puts where you currently are into perspective, helps you feel successful, and generates energy for you to keep moving toward your goals.

6 STEPS TO GET YOU JOURNALING:

1. Date each journal entry so you can see your progress over time. This can also help you recognize "journaling deserts" where it's been more than a little while since your last entry. Seeing this might move you to add to your journal again.
2. Your mind is the best place to find what you should be writing about, so spend a few minutes searching your thoughts before you start. Dig into any hurt or stuck places if they're sitting there on the surface, waiting for you to write about them. Another way to choose a per-

...is to do a quick review of the main areas of ...e home, work, family, and physical or mental ...if something in a particular area is bothering ...ht need your focus.

...e easy fill-in statements like, "I want to," or "I'm feeling," or even, "I think." You can write about what is happening in your life right now, or even tell a story. If you need or want more detailed writing prompts, you can find them online, and there are also 365-day prompt journals aplenty for sale.

4. To start, set a timer to write for five minutes and keep writing the entire time in whatever format or style works for you. You don't have to write in complete sentences, and you can use bullet points if that feels good to you. If you want to type in angry or excited ALL CAPS, have at it. Ditto for using a red or purple pen, and you can misspell anything you want.

5. Once you've finished your entry, take the time to read and absorb what you've written. Even if it does not immediately resonate with you, there may be something that you'll recall someday. It may be part of a solution for a future situation or problem.

6. Aim to journal at least a few times a week, and then build from there if it makes sense for you. Setting regular days and times will help you incorporate it into your schedule until it becomes routine, but don't feel pressured to write each day. This is one tool among many we'll review, and you'll need to make time for all the ones that work for you.

WRAP IT UP

Starting from a place of self-love brings power to your process of change. Partake in activities that encourage self-love and set boundaries so you can cater to your own needs. Journaling will help you express that love and release negativity so you can center yourself; it also provides you with a safe, non-judgmental place to reflect on where you've been and visualize where you're going.

Now that we've set the stage with journaling as an exercise to help you write about the major themes of this book (and beyond), consider when you can make time for yourself each day. Formally creating space for *you* is a building block for the base of healthy practices we'll explore in the next chapter. On the next step, we'll look at ways for you to use that time to get yourself and your surroundings in shape.

DO THE WORK

Here's where you'll think about, write about, and do the things that help you implement the lessons from each step. Dedicating a single place, like a notebook or document, for journaling and your work from this book can keep you organized and lets you look back on both as you progress through this process. Take the time you need to complete the work before you move on to the next chapter to reinforce what you've read and to be ready for the next step.

- What is your preferred method to document your journal entries? Typing or handwriting? If you prefer handwriting, get yourself a dedicated notebook, pad of paper, or journal.
- Think and write about the amount of self-love you're currently giving and your ability to set healthy boundaries. How can you improve on these if you feel the need?
- Write your love letter to yourself in whatever form you choose. Start by answering the questions listed earlier, and write beyond them if the words are flowing. Mail it to yourself when you're finished, and read it thoroughly when it arrives.
- Think and write about the changes you want to make, and consider which one is the most pressing to you right now.
- Start a regular journal practice, if you don't already have one, using the steps above.
- Do you feel like you're a perfectionist? If so, think and write about how it shows up for you. Begin to soften your stance on how "perfect" things need to be.

CHAPTER FIVE

STEP 2: LAY DOWN A STRONG BASE

I probably won't tell you much that you haven't already heard, but the healthy approaches and ideas in this chapter bear repeating and can positively impact your starting position. The question is, how many of them are you doing for yourself right now? Having a solid base will make it easier to add new practices to your life.

Have you ever tried going to the gym after having one too many glasses of wine the night before or not getting enough sleep? You know how important that workout is and how good it will make you feel, but you struggle to get there. You can force yourself to go, but the workout feels much harder because, physically, you're not in the best condition to take it on.

Deciding to make changes without being in the right head

and body space can feel like that workout. The path may be just as challenging. And the results might fall short of where they could have been had you been hydrated, well-rested, and better prepared overall.

As we climb this second step, we'll look at ways for you to attain your best state of health so you're ready to do the work that comes next. Set yourself up for success by scheduling time to devote to you, along with creating a clutter-free area around you. Aim for balance by fueling your body wisely, consistently getting a good night's sleep, being active, and developing an attitude of gratitude.

CREATE TIME IN YOUR DAY FOR YOU

What are the best times in your day that won't get over-taken by other people and their needs? What times can you earmark for the exercises and practices in this book? Is it first thing in the morning after coffee? Or maybe at night when the rest of the house has gone to bed? Rope off times in your mind you're most likely to commit to, when some-thing won't suddenly pop up and take away your attention or ability to focus on yourself.

Making time for you and the things you'll learn will allow you to be less stressed, more prepared for change, and hap-pier overall. It can positively impact every single aspect of your life. You'll be a better friend, mom, partner, and even pet owner if you carve out these times for yourself and use them for your own good.

The plan that seems to work best for most women is waking up a little earlier or arranging their morning routine so they can take time for themselves before the hustle of the day is upon them. I call it the "pay yourself first" approach. While this phrase usually refers to a financial investment strategy, here it's the idea of spending your energy on you first, before you expend it making everyone else's lives easier or better.

My morning includes a 5:45 a.m. wake-up call, which ensures I have time for quiet meditation and cardio while the house is still asleep. It's a workaround; if I don't get up early and take time for myself, I put everyone else's needs first. It allows me to set a tone of calm and peace for the day and helps me get clear on the things I want.

If the morning doesn't work for you to use the valuable tools we'll discuss, can you commit to another block of time midday, or even before you go to bed? If not, protect small segments of time throughout the day for yourself. Start with ten minutes in the morning or evening, take ten minutes around lunch to close the computer and put down your cell phone, and then find another ten minutes in the day if you can't put aside a single, larger stretch of time.

DECLUTTER YOUR SPACE

Removing things around you that no longer serve you will make room for new possibilities, help you find a new groove, and even welcome in new people to assist you in making changes. Our belongings can become heavy anchors around our necks, especially if they carry negative energy or memories that no longer have a place with us. Ditch the things that don't belong and surround yourself with items that bring you joy and energize you on the way to your newly changed life.

Dr. Sally Augustin, environmental psychologist and self-proclaimed "design shrink," is the author of *Designology: How to Find Your Place Type and Align Your Life with Design*. In this book, Dr. Augustin explains that having clutter around us, especially in our sight, negatively impacts our mental and physical wellness and puts us on edge. The more disorganization and clutter overall, the harder we have to work to hunt and pick through it to find the things we're looking for, and that can be stressful. To successfully make changes, you need to keep your confidence and enthusiasm high and your stress low, so give yourself a leg up and reduce your everyday anxiety by getting your surroundings in order.

Give her book a read if you're curious about the right way to decorate your space based on your personality, which also plays to your needs. The research-backed design suggestions are such a lovely blend of art and science, and having an appropriately furnished place in the context of making changes can enhance your mood and magnify your creativity. It's also meaningful for the things around you to be a true reflection of you.

Decluttering can give you a serious burst of energy to take on new challenges, and it has other positive benefits, too. It gives you confidence in your ability to make decisions and see a project through to the end and helps you enthusiastically take on your next task. Focusing on an easier chore—like purging—can also allow your mind to work on complex projects or problems in the background, which can lead to creative solutions.

My divorce left me with 12 years of clutter in my basement. Wedding pictures, my son's art projects, paperwork, and more from a life that no longer existed loomed in the back of my mind and needed to be cleaned up before I could truly move forward. I wouldn't let anyone see my mess. I was embarrassed of it, and there were times when I felt like the failure of my marriage and my life was hiding just below me.

It took me leaving my job and using my self-mandated time off to get through the clutter. I knew what was waiting for me. There was so much emotion wrapped up in the process of looking through it all—crying, letting go, and then enjoying the emotional and physical space it created.

I worked through every inch of it, throwing out or giving away items that no longer mattered, and then organizing everything else. It was only then that I was able to give new life to that space and use it for my loved ones. Most importantly, cleaning out my mental closet gave me the ability to begin exploring how my new life was going to look, and how I could help people and be fulfilled myself.

MAKE YOUR HEALTH A GOOD HABIT

Habits are defined as settled tendencies or practices that are hard to give up. They become ingrained and are such a part of our automatic behaviors that we hardly need to think about them to do them. The healthful tips on food, drink, sleep, and exercise given here are great permanent additions to give you the vitality you need to make changes now and beyond, rather than quick fixes that will eventually go by the wayside.

I've chosen to create good eating and drinking habits as fixtures in my life, as opposed to dieting or severely restricting what I consume for small periods of time to reach some temporary and arbitrary level of health. As you read these next sections, concentrate on the habits you can add or where you can adjust, to have far-reaching effects not only on your process of change, but also on your life. Treat these as essential ingredients in your life's pantry—ones you will always have on hand, and as the base of everything you do.

FOOD

Food is fuel for your body, so put in the premium grade to get the best results. My mantra regarding food and drink is nothing to excess, also known as everything in moderation. Nothing should be forbidden unless there's a medical reason for it, because putting things on the naughty list only makes you want them more.

My plan includes healthy eating and drinking by keeping sugar intake relatively low and having plenty of lean protein, greens, brown rice, and fruit in my meals. Semi-sweet chocolate chips satisfy my sweet tooth, and I sprinkle them on yogurt for an afternoon snack. Bread and pasta are delicious but make me feel doughy, so I try to keep them to a minimum. Pasta does make appearances during the week, but bread is usually exiled to dinners eaten out.

On weekdays, I try not to eat after 7:30 p.m. On the weekends, I allow myself to eat whatever I want, whenever I want. I'll have just about anything if I'm really craving it, but I tend not to gorge myself because unhealthy food makes me feel sluggish. Emphasize good over not-so-good-for-you food, and find the combo that helps you perform at your best.

DRINK

Our bodies are made up of 60% water on average, and

drinking it is vital for the functioning of our heart, brain, and muscles. Staying hydrated can ward off fatigue, which can make you feel dull and less likely to try new things, and it helps you think right and concentrate. Keep a cup or glass within reach and drink as much water as you can each day, without making yourself run to the bathroom every 20 minutes.

Coffee, tea, and other beverages do hydrate, but water does it so much better. Hot green tea is my constant companion—it has less caffeine and creates less of the jitters than coffee, but still has enough to rev up your brain function. It also has bioactive compounds that promote good health along with anti-anxiety properties. Watch the syrup and leave out the whipped cream if coffee is your go-to, and keep fruit juice to a minimum because it's loaded with sugar.

Adding green juice to my diet in the morning was pivotal. Fresh-pressed celery juice had become widely available, so I gave it a try and found out it's full of vitamins and minerals, has more than 20 anti-inflammatory compounds, and helps keep you well-hydrated since it's about 95% water. I had just begun meditating, and between that and the morning juice, I had loads of energy and a deepened sense of focus and calm.

You can control what goes into your juice by using an at-home juicer. The investment is relatively low for something of such quality, and using organic fruit and veggies rather than store-bought juices means you'll recoup your spend in no time. Kale, celery, cucumber, red pepper, fresh ginger, and lemon is my standard blend, but the combinations are endless, and you'll feel an almost immediate uptick in your vigor from juicing. If buying pre-made juice works better for you, read the ingredients so you know what you're getting, and keep the fruit and sugar to a minimum.

Keep alcohol consumption under control to wake up feeling refreshed with a clear head and your motivation high. The *2015-2020 Dietary Guidelines for Americans* (from the U.S. Department of Health and Human Services and U.S. Department of Agriculture), defines moderate alcohol consumption as one drink per day for women, and up to two drinks per day for men. And no, you can't "bank" them during the week and drink them all together over the weekend.

SLEEP

Adults need seven to nine hours of sleep each night, but most of us don't get it. We're being sucked in by media (social and otherwise), working too much, not climbing into bed early enough and not without having some sort of screen in front us. In the context of preparing to make changes, not getting the right amount of sleep leads to more negative emotions during the day and makes it harder to see things in a positive light.

Develop good sleep habits if you don't already have them. Put down your phone and turn off your computer or TV at least 30 minutes before you get into bed. Choose another way to wind down, like reading a physical book (not an e-book), journaling, or even connecting with your significant other if you have one. Nothing beats real, human connection, and you'll need their support in the very near future.

EXERCISE

Exercise, even a brisk walk, should make its way into your everyday life. Regular physical activity creates a lasting sense of well-being. It also reduces stress and anxiety by increasing your brain's production of endorphins, the neurotransmitters that elevate our overall feeling of pleasure and give us a natural high.

The good news about exercise continues, as it can increase self-confidence and decrease feelings of mild depression, help you relax, and even help you sleep. Making changes can certainly be anxiety provoking, so get into a daily routine of raising your heart rate in ways you enjoy so you're motivated to do it. It's even better if you can commune with nature at the same time.

Make small tweaks in your day to sprinkle in movement if you can't find a single chunk of time to dedicate to a workout. Easy adjustments like parking far away from the entrance to the grocery store, taking stairs instead of an elevator, and taking a walk break for even five minutes every hour get your blood pumping and the brain-boosting juices flowing. Even standing rather than sitting while you work burns more calories, makes you more mentally alert, and improves your outlook.

BALANCE AS BEST YOU CAN

Balance is fluid; it's not something you can set and forget. Listen to what your body says it needs, and use that to find the right mix of good behavior for you. Balance can also be fleeting, and what works for you one week or month may not work the next, so take notice when you're feeling off and be prepared to continuously seek better balance.

My boyfriend says that I have a "delicate ecosystem." If I'm getting enough sleep and eating properly, along with exercising and finding time to meditate, all is right in my world and I can nearly levitate from the amount of energy I have. When I'm super stressed and out of balance, eating too much junk food and not working out, the world suffers with me. It's just who I am, but I've learned how important these things are for my ability to show up with the mindset and determination I need to get things done.

HAVE AN ATTITUDE OF GRATITUDE

Put the written work from your love letter to yourself into practice by focusing on what you're grateful for. Begin each day with gratitude for the things you've identified in yourself and in your life; focus on your strengths and the simple pleasures surrounding you. The good vibes that come from this daily practice will help you move forward to your next phase.

You can sneak this in before getting out of bed in the morning, while you're showering or brushing your teeth, or even when you're driving to work. You don't need to formally sit down with yourself to practice this unless you absolutely want to. Notice how this shift to being thankful first thing in the morning sets a positive tone for the day.

Being grateful throughout your day, even in frustrating situations and with unhappy people, will draw positivity to you and create an uplifted platform for change in you. Annoy your family and friends with the number of times you thank them for the small things and for just being who they are. Little do they know the gift and power of positivity they're receiving from you.

WRAP IT UP

Making yourself a priority, tidying up your place, and putting yourself in your best possible physical health will create a strong foundation to work from as you move through the next steps. Eat and drink well, get good sleep, and get your heart pumping with exercise to feel your best and to boost your confidence level. Fill your days with gratitude for all that you are and all that you have.

Now that you've learned to swap that extra glass of wine for a glass of water (or know that you'll pay for it the next day if you don't), we'll elaborate on positivity and its importance as you look to make changes. Your personal energy and level of belief have serious consequences as to what you can accomplish and have in your life. On Step 3, we'll walk through ways to keep them high and help you begin to see the guideposts being set out for you.

DO THE WORK

- When can you make uninterrupted time each day for the important activities that will support your change? If it's not in a single session, consider and write down how you can accumulate at least 30 minutes total in smaller increments for yourself.
- Declutter your space.
- Log everything you eat and drink and how much sleep and exercise you get each day for a week to find opportunities to be better. Review and write the positive changes you can make for yourself with the following:
  - Food and drink (non-alcoholic)
  - Alcohol consumption

- ◦ Sleep
- ◦ Exercise
- Give green juice a try if it's not something you're already drinking. Small amounts of fruit juice can significantly adjust the taste if you need it. If you already drink green juice, consider buying a juicer.
- Get your heart rate up every day by working out or adding walks and stair climbing to your routine.
- Be grateful for at least three things each morning and actively practice gratitude throughout the day. Work to find ways to be thankful even with challenging situations or people.

CHAPTER SIX

STEP 3: POSITIVITY AND OPTIMISM ARE NOT DIRTY WORDS

Being rear-ended in my car was not how I thought I'd be shown the way, but there it was. I believed I could find my true path and had generated as much positive energy as possible to find my next adventure after I left my career behind. I openly consulted the universe as I considered going to grad school at the age of 46, and my answer was a bright red sign that said WRONG WAY in the form of a car accident. If you ask for guidance and then pay attention, sometimes the message is just that clear.

On this third step up your stairway, we'll expand your preparation and mindset to include positivity and optimism as powerful weapons in your arsenal for change. We'll explore the Law of Attraction and how you can use your positive energy, actions, and thoughts to bring the good things you want into your life. Then we'll look at how coincidences and synchronicities can help point you in the right direction.

WHAT THE #@$!?

There is this weird thing that happened with self-help books shortly after 2010. Maybe you noticed it too, and you might have even read some of them. They have swear words in the title and start with the premise that you're broken, seemingly beyond belief, and then give you advice so you can try to fix yourself, or maybe find a way to embrace your brokenness so it feels like it's part of the norm.

Clearly, this is not one of those books. Here's the truth: you put yourself into your own hole if you believe you're in that bad of shape. Everyone has good days and bad days, suffers loss, and struggles through hard times whether they let you see it or not. *Everyone has something they deal with, every single day.*

Knowing that, you should revel in the fact that you've decided to make it different. You've moved past the point of thinking you're beyond repair and have elevated yourself by being right here, right now. You're preparing to make changes and should be immensely proud of yourself and the person you are.

Even though the book I'm about to mention seems to fall into that "other" category, it's actually one of the good ones, with a positive curse word in the title and a better attitude. I have much love for Jen Sincero and *You Are A Badass: How to Stop Doubting Your Greatness and Start Living an Awesome Life*, which randomly made its way into my hands on a BBQ-filled trip to Austin, Texas. She upped the cool factor of the modern self-help era with her self-deprecating and "hell yes" approach, and she should get props for it. Her book is also extremely entertaining and starts with the premise that you're amazing—not broken.

LET YOUR POSITIVITY REIGN

Rising above the negativity surrounding you and learning to overcome your own pessimistic thoughts and internal dialogue will make space for good energy in your days. I became known as a princess of positivity just before my exodus from corporate America. I knew there was a better life waiting. That conviction, an unstoppable attitude, and hard mental work helped me find the right way to it.

Having a high level of belief in what you can do and the devotion to doing it is a powerful combination for getting exactly what you want. If you think you can't have the good things you want in your life, you never will. That kind of limited thinking is more toxic to your dreams than smoking or sitting.

Start thinking about what you want and imagine what your life will feel like once you have it. The more detailed the images you create, and the more you can feel the positive impact it will make, the more heightened the enthusiasm and energy you'll produce. Use it to make your new future a reality.

This kind of visualization works well with the gratitude exercises from the previous chapter. First, be grateful for the life you have right now, and then move on to see and feel how much better life will be once you make changes. You don't need to wait until you know how to get to where you want to start believing you can get there. Allow your mind to focus on the end result.

As you're gearing up for your change, you may need to adjust your vocabulary. Saying or thinking things like "I can't" sets up mental barriers to change. Instead, think or say, "I'm working on it," or, "I will eventually."

Let go of the "no" and open yourself up to numerous possibilities. Pay attention to your thoughts and words and actively correct yourself. Shift your internal and external dialogue to something more positive when negativity sneaks in.

POSITIVITY IS GOOD, OPTIMISM IS EVEN BETTER

Optimism takes positivity a step further by adding confidence that there will be a successful end. Optimists are defined as people who anticipate positive outcomes, whether serendipitously or through perseverance and effort, and who are confident of attaining desired goals. Serendipity just might be one of the most uplifting words to describe a happy chance, and an optimist's life is full of them.

Optimists tend to view negative outcomes as learning experiences. They also see them as being temporary, specific to the instance, and due to external circumstances rather than blaming themselves for what went wrong. Because of this mentality, they're more likely to see the potential for change.

Optimistic people are more likely to do the work that needs to be done and are less likely to give up before they reach their goals. Gabriele Oettingen, professor of psychology at New York University, succinctly said, "High optimism will predict high effort and success." It sounds pretty simple. Do the work, expect it will pay off, and it will.

Another plus for optimists is that they're generally healthier and less stressed. They're more likely to take risks for larger payoffs and tend to live longer. If you're not already a natural optimist, are you wondering how you can be?

6 STEPS TO BEING MORE OPTIMISTIC:

1. Recognize your negative thoughts. They tend to entail

putting yourself down, doubting your abilities, criticizing yourself when you make mistakes, expecting failure, and fearing the future. Pay attention to your inner thoughts as you think about or encounter stressful situations and write them down. Review them and check for negative patterns.

2. Challenge your negative thoughts with a little self-love and some reasonable expectations to see if you're being unfair and unkind to yourself. Imagine that a good friend had the same thoughts and asked you to comment on them. What would you say?

3. Train your brain to counteract negative thoughts and talk by immediately thinking or saying something positive. Negate them both with forward-looking affirmations, using power words like "can," "commit," and "confident." If you think or say, "I'll never be able to make this change," stop yourself and the flow of negativity. Take a deep breath. Then think or say, "I'm committed to doing the hard work and making this happen." Allow yourself the time to feel the positivity that reverberates through you when you do.

4. Believe in your possibility for change and develop a regular routine of writing down positive messages, thoughts, and emotions. Your journal is a perfect place for this.

5. Practice gratitude every day.

6. Be mindful. Work to focus on exactly what you're doing, when you're doing it. (You'll learn more about mindfulness on the next step.)

ATTRACT WHAT YOU WANT WITH
THE LAW OF ATTRACTION

The Law of Attraction is said to be a law of the universe, like gravity. It's always working, whether you know about it and believe in it, and regardless of whether you actively use it or not. It uses the attractive, magnetic power of the universe. The basic premise is that like attracts like, positivity attracts positivity, and negativity attracts negativity. Your positive or negative beliefs, thoughts, words, and actions can bring positive or negative experiences into your life.

If you're reading about the Law of Attraction for the first time, it may feel like a stretch, but there are plenty of books on the subject and some science to back it up. My first exposure to its underlying concepts came from Deepak Chopra's book, *The Spontaneous Fulfillment of Desire: Harnessing the Infinite Power of Coincidence*. Reading this self-help book was an epiphany and showed up at exactly the right time in my life, when I knew I wanted more for myself. And that was quite a coincidence.

That being said, there is mystery and a little intrigue surrounding the Law of Attraction. Some argue that it's always been in existence, and that Jesus, Buddha, and many other religious and spiritual figures of the world have used its concepts in their work and teachings. The first extensive and formal writing about the Law came in the late 1800s, in a book called *Thoughts Are Things,* written by Prentice

Mulford. He was an important figure in the New Thought philosophy, which has been called a religion of healthy mindedness.

The Law of Attraction ties in with some concepts we've already explored and focuses on both raising your personal energetic frequency and tapping into the vibrational energy of the universe to manifest the things you want. The word "manifest" can have a New Age-y, hocus-pocus connotation, but the scientist in me geeks out on the quantum physics used to explain it all.

Ultimately, our ability to attract good, positive things that resonate at a higher vibration comes from the practice of raising our own energy and vibrations to match them. By doing this, along with clearly setting intentions for what we think we can truly attain and continuously exploring the future fantastic feelings of attaining it, we energetically create our path to it. You don't need to understand the exact science behind the Law of Attraction to put it to use and attract what you want.

12 EASY WAYS TO RAISE YOUR ENERGY AND VIBRATION

Our thoughts are pure energy. Keeping them and yourself positive, uplifted, and happy is the name of the game. These actions are easy to do and many will sound familiar.

1. Have a morning ritual to set a positive tone for the day. Be grateful and optimistic.
2. Take time to visualize the things you want and feel how marvelous your life will be once you have them.
3. Journal about what you want to draw into your life; be specific and include details!
4. Move your body. Get up and stretch when you've been sitting too long. Raise your heart rate by walking and doing cardio.
5. Properly fuel your body by eating and drinking healthy foods.
6. Read and watch what inspires you most. Yes, inspirational quotes count.
7. Turn on and turn up the music. Sing and dance too, if you're feeling it.
8. Smile, laugh, be silly, hug, and connect in every possible way with the people you love.
9. Spend as much time outdoors with nature as you can.
10. Do fun, creative activities that you personally enjoy. Adult coloring books are available in checkout lanes, and wine and painting are a great pairing. If you can sew, knit, or crochet, I'm in awe of you.
11. Nap. A cup of tea or coffee followed by a 20-minute mid-day catnap will reenergize you.
12. Use essential oils. Each has its own benefits, and many have both energizing and calming abilities. Use in a diffuser, apply to your wrist, or use in a bath. Eucalyptus, lemon, and bergamot oil (the citrus note in Earl Grey

tea), are my three favorites. (Always check the label to see if they're safe for use in direct contact with skin.)

To use the Law of Attraction in this process, start by visualizing what you want and feeling what it will be like to have it. Think optimistic and uplifting thoughts, put as much good out into the world as possible with your actions, and pass along positive energy to everyone you come into contact with, regardless of their disposition. You'll get back what you give, and these acts together will amplify your ability to effect change and create the life you want.

Remember that spectacular guy I willed into being? I could have just as easily said I "manifested" him. High-five to the Law of Attraction for bringing him into my life.

COINCIDENCES AND SYNCHRONICITIES: PAY ATTENTION FOR DIRECTION

Now that you're setting your intentions for change by visualizing how phenomenal your life will be in the not-too-distant future and working toward positive thoughts, actions, and talk, start paying attention to the signs you're being given. Coincidences are defined as occasions when two or more similar things happen at the same time, especially in a way that is unlikely and surprising. Coincidences that line up with what you're working to attract are synchronicities, and they can be powerful messages that show how you should proceed.

Pay close attention to what you're seeing, hearing, and feeling; even search for meaning in the most unsuspecting places, like accidents. Discover the directives you're getting from the world around you. You may see similar images, hear the same words or phrases being repeated, deeply connect with a specific place, or even hear the same song play over and over. These messages can help point the way and give you direction in planning your next steps.

People can be signs of synchronicity, too, and new ones may come into your life to help guide you at this time. They might have made the changes you want to make, have advice or support to offer, or may be a principal player in helping you get to where you want to be. There's an appropriate quote that one of my clients shared with me: "When the student is ready, the teacher will appear." Its exact origins are up for debate, but the message is powerful and clear.

I'm grateful and honored that she used this quote in regard to me and our work together. What a wonderful seal of approval from the universe that I've found my calling and that I'm doing exactly what I'm supposed to be doing.

WRAP IT UP

All the hard work in the world can fall flat if there's not also an overwhelming belief that you can, and will, have the things you want. Be an optimist. Visualize how fulfilling your life will be when you make changes and how good it will feel once you have.

Keep your thoughts, feelings, and interactions positive and your personal energy high. You'll begin to attract the good things you want most by using the Law of Attraction, and the universe will be there with a roadmap for you to follow. You simply need to pay close attention to what it's telling you about how to proceed.

I didn't get hit by a truck of change. Instead, I got a synchronistic jolt from the messenger car of the universe when I asked for a signal about going back to school. A wrong way sign can be as impactful as a green light in your life—you just need to heed what you're being shown. Meditation and mindfulness are powerful practices that can help you focus and give you clarity to receive the directions you're being given; you'll learn about these next.

DO THE WORK

- Visualize how you want your life to look in the future. Feel how happy, fulfilled, and enthusiastic you will be. Combine this with your gratitude practice.
- Work to be more optimistic by writing out positive messages when journaling about your positive thoughts and emotions.
- Recognize and record your negative thoughts for a week,

then review them to see if there are patterns that emerge. Employ self-love and actively work on changing your inner thoughts and talk to something more uplifting.

- Put positive thoughts, actions, and feelings out into the world.
- Keep your vibration levels high by using your favorite energy-boosting activities each day.
- Think and write about coincidences. Do they happen with regularity for you?
- Watch for synchronicities that dovetail with change and pay attention to what they're telling you.

CHAPTER SEVEN

STEP 4: MINDFULNESS AND MEDITATION WILL CHANGE YOUR LIFE

We as a society are ridiculously stressed and anxiety-ridden, and it's only getting worse. The 2018 Stress in America™ Survey from the American Psychological Association revealed that nearly 75% of adults reported physical or emotional symptoms of stress, and almost half say it has kept them awake at night. It's probably no surprise that being a woman puts you in a higher-risk category for all of it.

My running joke and commentary about this sad state of society is that "even my dog has anxiety." He's a rescue Husky mix and it's pretty common with his kind, but I do tend to attract the people (and apparently dogs) that need my help the most. When I find that someone is struggling with stress, my first suggestion is for them to bring mindfulness and meditation to their days to help ease their strain.

The goal of Step 4 is to present easy ways for you to add mindfulness and meditation to your routine. Like the lessons you've learned so far, finding and sticking to a set time each day will cement these tools into your way of life, plus give you the emotional strength and sense of balance you need during change. They demand for you to be present, so you can concentrate on the things you want moving forward.

If these are already a part of what you do, good for you! Keep it up. Work to expand the frequency of these practices if you can. You have an effective framework for finding peace and calm and making space to visualize and feel how your positive changes will impact you. If not, know that these are game changers and get ready to be astounded.

HOW MINDFULNESS AND MEDITATION HELP

Mindfulness and meditation go hand in hand, but they're not the same. Mindfulness is a state of awareness; it can be practiced everywhere and anywhere by being fully present in exactly what you're doing at that very minute. Meditation tends to be done in a specific place or way, for set periods of time, often centering on developing focus and clarity. The benefits of mindfulness and meditation cannot be denied, and it's clear we need them now more than ever.

Having mindfulness and meditation in your life can increase positive emotions and promote a sense of well-being, plus reduce negative emotions and stress. More specifically, by using mindfulness and meditation, you can amp up your immune system, get more restful sleep, be better equipped to tune out distractions, and have improved memory and attention skills. Practicing mindfulness and meditation may also slow the aging process and be as powerful as antidepressants to help combat depression.

People who develop the practices of mindfulness and meditation have a stronger sense of self, including a healthier body image and higher self-esteem. They're more resilient when faced with negativity from other people. They also tend to have healthier relationships overall, including a greater sense of compassion for themselves and others.

Incorporating these practices into your life can literally alter your brain structure by thickening and strengthening the specific areas associated with focus, organization, planning, emotional regulation, and memory. And the results aren't just in our head; there is proof positive of these physical changes. Using an MRI, you can see and measure the increase in brain density that comes with using them.

Meditation and mindfulness are referred to as "practices" because they'll never be perfect. If you have a little perfectionist living inside of you, you'll need to put her on the shelf. But, like physical exercise, with repetition you can develop a type of mental memory that helps you get started more easily and find your center more quickly.

MINDFULNESS

Mindfulness is a mental state achieved by concentrating our awareness on the present, while calmly acknowledging and accepting our feelings, thoughts, and body sensations. When we practice it, we zero in on the present and what we're sensing right now, rather than dwelling on the past or worrying about the future. Once you get the hang of it, this can be your quickie go-to that helps you focus and relieve stress.

It can be hard for us to be in the here and now when we're so chronically overscheduled. We're busy rehashing conversations from earlier in the day or keeping track of what comes next once we're done with the things we're in the middle of doing, all the while worrying about how to prepare for tomorrow's meeting, and so on. Taking mindfulness breaks throughout the day will give you the mental pause you need to be present and stay vibrant.

HOW TO PRACTICE MINDFULNESS

To practice mindfulness, keep your attention on this very moment and what you're thinking and feeling without judgment. Be present and don't replay the events of the day or put together a laundry list of things to do. Pay attention to the thoughts that pop into your head along with what you feel in your body, and make a mental note to follow up with yourself on anything that surprises you or needs a closer look.

I actively practice mindfulness while I wash dishes, empty or fill the dishwasher, and fold clothes. They are simple and satisfying activities that allow me to quickly check in with myself. They also have a clearly defined process that brings order to chaos (which I crave) and helps me keep the space around me uncluttered.

Another easy way to practice mindfulness is by taking a walk. Be aware of your breath, feel how your feet hit the ground as you step forward, and work to keep your mind clear of all things that are not in that very moment. Walks in nature or in the woods can help enhance the feeling of relation with everything and everyone around you, and increase your feelings of peace and calm.

MEDITATION

Meditation has documented origins in India around 1500 BCE and in China in 600-500 BCE, but it's believed to have been practiced as early as 3000 BCE. It has roots in many different cultures and religions, including Judaism, Hinduism, Taoism, and Buddhism, among others. There's a rich and long history of people from all over the world and in all walks of life using different types of meditation to achieve focus, relief from stress, inner peace, calm and relaxation, and even insight to the connectedness of the universe.

While meditating, you focus your attention on something, such as your breath, an emotional connection with yourself and others, physical sensations of different parts of your body, sounds, visualized images, and more. There are many different types of meditation, and you should choose the one that feels right to you—one you can easily do, and will continue to do on a regular basis.

Yoga, which means "to unite," combines physical movement, breath, and meditation to promote unity of the mind and body. I mention it here because its intent is to help you find peace and harmony with yourself and the universe, and it's much more than a form of physical exercise. Your dance card of healthy mind and body activities is filling up, but you should explore and add this to your preparation if you have interest and the time to do it.

There is no single best way to meditate. It's incredibly personal and may change for you depending on the day, where you are mentally, and what you need. Know that not all meditation sessions are created equal, and you may combine several techniques to find the exact focus you're looking for.

"HOW DO I MEDITATE?"

When I made the all-important choice to meditate over medicating in my marriage therapist's living room, I really had no idea how to do it. I Googled "How do I meditate?" and the Wildmind website was the first place I went. The name was appropriate; I needed help to calm my own wild mind and to stop the rubber ball of random thoughts and self-criticism that was constantly bouncing around in my head.

I adopted the mindfulness of breathing meditation that very day. It was quick to learn and easy for me to do. I suggest this method to friends, family, and clients that are curious about how to get started.

5 STEPS TO START MEDITATING - MINDFULNESS OF BREATHING:

1. Sit or lie in a comfortable position on the floor, in a chair, or on a couch, wherever you are most likely to relax. If you can cross your legs in a traditional lotus position, where each foot is placed on the opposite thigh, great. If you would rather sit or lay with your legs straight and have a blanket over you, do it. Pillows can also help

support you. There is no wrong way to set yourself up; do what feels best for you.

2. Choose a number to count to. Fifty is a good starting point; you can always increase the number if necessary.

3. Close your eyes and focus on your breath. Deeply inhale through your nose, then deeply exhale again through your nose, noticing the coolness of the air rushing around your nostrils as you breathe in, and the warm air rushing out as you exhale. Then count each breath in your mind. Count to your chosen number, and if you lose track, just start over.

4. Once you hit your number, switch the order of breathing and counting and start again. Count the number first, then deeply inhale and deeply exhale through your nose, noticing the same sensations as before. Count again to your chosen number.

5. Once you finish the second set, stop counting and concentrate entirely on your breathing. Stay with this focus and feeling until your session is over to help quiet your mind and gain a sense of calm.

You may also want to try guided meditation where you are led by someone else's voice. Websites and apps like Headspace, The Mindfulness App, and Calm allow you to customize your session based on your needs and what you're trying to attain. There are also in-person group and online group meditations that use a guide and should not be missed. The collective energy that comes from the gathering is something that needs to be experienced as it can hardly be explained.

The amount of time you devote to your practice is your decision. Longer sessions can bring a deeper sense of peace and tranquility, but if you only have ten minutes before your daily life wakes up and starts demanding things of you, take it. Aim for three to five-minute increments in the very beginning, and increase from there when you're ready.

I've read that 30 minutes is an optimal amount of time to meditate, but my lucky number is 13 minutes on a good day. Consistency beats length, so set a time and place each day when you can grab a few minutes of quiet. Eventually, you'll be able to meditate almost anywhere. (I meditate through takeoff when I fly alone because it's the scariest part for me.)

On some days, your mind will simply want to wander. When this happens, be kind to yourself, reset, and recenter. When all else fails, because sometimes it will and that's okay, you can always come back to your breath and begin again.

MANTRA MEDITATION

Mantra meditation can be a logical progression after you've gotten comfortable with mindfulness of breathing meditation. A mantra is a repeated word or phrase and can help improve your concentration. To try this, you'll need to find words or phrases that resonate with you.

After I found focus through counting, I moved on to using the Hindu mantra "So Hum," meaning "I am," and still use it today. It supports self-love and the fact that you're enough, being exactly who you are, and where you are in life. To use this mantra for meditation, breathe in and think "So" and breathe out and think "Hum," concentrating on your breath and losing yourself in the words as you repeat them over and over.

You can also use words for the things you want to attract. Three is my favorite number, so I used the mantra "family, free time, fulfillment" as I made the decision to leave my career behind and spend more time with my son, get control of my life, and follow my calling. The words "creativity, connection, completion" moved me along as I wrote this book.

MORE MEDITATION TECHNIQUES TO TRY

Visualization and resting awareness meditation use a specific thing or place to direct your focus and help you acknowledge, and then remove, the thoughts that come up. I use the mountains of Arizona or a clear, light blue sky as a starting place and visualize my thoughts as clouds that have drifted into the scene. I dissolve the clouds and the thoughts in my mind and return to the cloudless sun-drenched sky.

Loving-kindness or compassion meditation can help you let go of negativity or unhappiness with yourself or with others. Begin with positive feelings and warm loving energy toward yourself that emanates from your heart. Imagine expanding the feelings to other people you know, then expand beyond that group and share the same feelings progressively outward with all the people in your town or city, then state, then country and beyond.

Sound bath meditation envelops you in the vibrations created by instruments made of different materials such as gongs, metal singing bowls, crystal bowls, chimes, and drums. It can help you relax and reduce stress by stimulating delta brainwaves that trigger the deep meditative state found during dreamless sleep. This state encourages cleansing and healing to help you release pent-up emotions. You may feel overwhelmingly happy or profoundly sad or completely nod off and wake up feeling incredibly refreshed.

People who have difficulty with more conventional practices may have an easier time finding serenity using sound. Each session will bring different results based on the person leading it and the instruments they're using, and of course, you. This is another not-to-be-missed in-person group activity, but you can participate in online virtual baths, using headphones for maximum effect.

BLOCK OUT NEGATIVITY

When you're putting in the work to be positive, it's important to protect yourself from the negativity around you. I attract people who need my help and take on negativity like velvet picks up dog hair. I can get hit with other people's bad energy or state of mind the minute they walk into a room, so I've incorporated a visualization in my meditation practice to protect myself from it.

Once I'm relaxed and focused, I surround myself in a bubble of light that acts like a force field. I imagine myself on a beach, under a sun so bright that everything else is nearly white. I envision an even brighter sphere of light being created around me, starting at my head, ballooning out and down on all sides at the same time, and finishing under my feet. This allows the good energy through but keeps other people's bad juju on the outside. This visualization is a great add-on, especially if you are close to toxic people you can't easily avoid or let go.

WRAP IT UP

The claim that mindfulness and meditation will change your life may sound a little overblown, but their impact on my life as I began to make changes to find my equanimity and happiness can't be overemphasized. Their transformative powers cannot be denied. These two practices alone can reduce your stress and anxiety and are some of the most powerful tools in your toolbox of preparation.

Leaving your racing thoughts and self-judgment behind by practicing mindfulness will help you quickly center yourself and can be done anywhere, at any time. Finding the easiest ways to silence your mind during regular meditation sessions will make space for possibility thinking and change. Getting comfortable with these life-changing practices and building them into your plan will prepare you to take the next step, go deeper, and learn to trust and rely on your inner voice to guide you.

DO THE WORK

- Find time each day to practice mindfulness. Notice what comes up when you do and think and write more deeply on it.
- Consider the best way to begin meditating if you haven't done it before. Would you prefer to be guided or to guide yourself through the practice?
- If you currently have a meditation practice, think about how you can expand it. Are there new approaches you'd like to try?
- Commit to a schedule of meditation with specific days and times and write it down. Add days, make your sessions longer, and try new techniques as you get more comfortable.

CHAPTER EIGHT

STEP 5: USE YOUR INNER VOICE TO MAKE CHANGES WITH CONFIDENCE

The thought of making a major change in your life, like leaving your job, can set off your internal alarm even if you know deep down you just can't stay there a minute longer. Your first instinct might be a big, fat "I CAN'T" in your mind, followed by a litany of excuses as to why not. You may even have conversations like this with yourself time and again without realizing it's only your personal protective mechanism speaking to you, and that once you push past it, you can find the next steps to take.

As you continue up onto the fifth stair of six in phase one, you'll learn to distinguish between your inner voice that will point you in the right direction, and your ego, which brings fear and control. I'll help you recognize your inner voice, and we'll look at different ways for you to connect with it. Hearing, trusting, and following through on what your inner voice is telling you can give you clear direction and confidence in your decisions, including how to make important changes.

WHAT IS YOUR INNER VOICE?

Inner voice, or intuition, is defined as the ability to understand something immediately, which comes from instinctive feeling rather than conscious reasoning. Also known as our sixth sense, it uses our personality and values, along with a split-second analysis of emotions, experiences, and perceptions, to warn us of danger or urge us toward things that are good for us. Research shows it comes from multiple areas in our brain associated with memory and emotion-based learning. It's informed by the pleasure of rewards and pain from mistakes of the past.

Your inner voice is the key to your personal truth, and it will guide you to your true answers. It may be a calm and clear voice in your head or even appear in your mind as words being projected on a screen. It's been described as a gut feeling that is uplifting and positive, or heavy and negative in response to something you're considering or have already done. It can also feel like tingling energy in your hands or at the back of your neck, or as a spreading warmth or heaviness across your solar plexus, chest, or in your heart, depending on whether you are being guided to or away from something.

Have you ever come to a decision and then had a sinking feeling or pit in your stomach that was later affirmed because it turned out to be the wrong decision? Or have you ever felt that a resolution was so right, like a final puzzle piece that linked everything together? Those feelings are your inner voice, compelling you to make decisions that line up with your beliefs and bring you happiness.

I stumbled upon my inner voice when I was in my early teens. I would zone out and get lost in my mind, working through things that felt unsettled or needed a decision, and answers would come to me. I could hear them in my head, and I'd type them out with my fingers on an imaginary typewriter. How you perceive your inner voice might be wildly different; it's an individual experience, and it may change as you get better acquainted with it.

IS THAT YOUR INNER VOICE OR YOUR EGO TALKING?

Pay close attention to what comes up when you're pondering a question or examining a situation. Your inner voice's response takes you wholly into account. Your ego, on the other hand, responds through the lens of reason, other people's views, and a whole bunch of other junk that will only get in the way of finding the right way for you.

Your inner voice and how you hear, feel, or see it is unique to you. If you do hear it, it tends to come across with a slow and knowing, confident, uplifting voice. It feels like it emanates from your heart or from deep inside of you.

Breathing deeply, finding a peaceful space for thought, being mindful, and meditating can all connect you with your inner voice. This will also help silence your ego, the louder, chattier voice in your head that makes decisions from a place of fear and hurt. The ego's job is to protect you, so it pushes back on things that are new or different. Since you're being moved to make changes, you'll want it out of the picture.

The English word "ego" is the Latin word for "I." It is your conscious mind, your sense of self, and it should sound awfully familiar to you. If you're not deeply connected with your inner voice, your ego can pop up as the first loud and bossy voice you hear when you're searching for answers.

Your ego is your inner critic and brings with it a false sense of urgency and impatience. It can feel tense and strained when it's speaking to you. Learn to quiet it and focus on your inner voice instead. You may also choose to tune into your ego, hear its message, and then look for your truth beyond it.

Direction from your ego comes from your head and it uses logic to argue with you. It makes you feel like you don't or won't have enough, like you're always in need, and it urges you to compete for and pursue external results like money and success to find happiness. Your inner voice, in contrast, knows you're enough and encourages you to enjoy all that you already have and to celebrate the greatness that comes from within you.

Letting go of your attachment to material things and knowing you'll have abundance in light of your change will help in setting you free from the ego's hold. This was one of my biggest hurdles to overcome in leaving my career behind. Yes, it was draining the joy out of me, but the dependence on money and the fear of never having enough kept me there for too many years.

6 STEPS TO HELP YOU FIND YOUR INNER VOICE:

1. Start by meditating or actively practicing mindfulness. Even a quick session for three minutes will do.
2. Focus on a specific situation you are considering. Ask a yes or no question about it in your mind.
3. Take a deep breath and mentally respond to your question with a yes. Take note of how you immediately feel and what comes up in your body when you do. Then take a deep breath and respond with a no and take note of your immediate response again.

4. Consider the sensations you received for both. A lifting, light, and energizing feeling goes along with the correct answer for you. Incorrect answers can bring weighty, negative, or tight feelings.

5. Write down the details and focus on your body's responses. Repeat and review these exercises to see the patterns that emerge around how you perceive your inner voice.

6. Work to become aware of things that suddenly flash in your mind, or inciteful feelings that come up during your day. Do not dismiss fleeting thoughts. Give them attention, notice what they're telling you, and jot them down.

HOW TO USE YOUR INNER VOICE

Once you "hear" your inner voice, there are several ways you can connect with it. Focus on a situation you want to change and then think about the possible solutions or outcomes, one at a time. Your inner voice will respond affirmatively to the right answer for you. For some, the response is a spoken or visual yes, and for others it is a feeling of increased energy, lightness, or warmth, wherever you experience it. Ideas not aligned with your highest purpose and authentic self will be dismissed by your inner voice with a no, or can feel ominous or heavy, and just won't sit well with you.

Another approach is to put the question or situation in the back of your mind. I call this "simmering on the backburner," and it's quite like the process we talked about when you declutter. Go about your business and try not to consciously find an answer to your question at hand; with time and space, imaginative solutions can emerge.

I connect with my inner voice during a workout (using the secondhand rowing machine in my decluttered basement) and, curiously enough, when I take a shower—when I'm not actively and forcefully trying to figure something out. I tell people I need to "shower on it" when a decision or solution is not easily coming to me. When I do, my slow and calm inner voice speaks to me and interesting ideas tend to appear. As I wrote this book, I often found myself jumping out of the shower and running to make notes to capture my thoughts.

In my previous career, I was fortunate to have been involved in the interview process for almost every hire. I didn't ask brilliant questions that revealed the true character of the person; I just had a keen sense of intuition that helped me decide whether or not they were going to be a good fit for our company. Beyond the interviews where the candidate was obviously not qualified, my inner voice would sound the alarm and I would get a negative, creeping feeling within the first few minutes if there was reason to be concerned about extending an offer, regardless of what was on their resume.

Managers invited me to sit in on their interviews and then

asked how I felt as soon as it was over. I'm grateful to have been part of a supportive workplace that allowed me to openly express my gut feelings; I was able to use and trust my inner voice at a very early stage in my career. It also helped me recognize when it was time to go at the end of it.

LEARN TO TRUST YOUR INNER VOICE

With practice, your inner voice can become a clear advisor. The more you learn to call upon it, the stronger it will be. The more you trust in its ability to guide you, the more empowered you will become.

In turn, you'll learn to trust yourself and have the utmost confidence in the decisions you make. You will just know they're right for you. Be invigorated by the new road that is emerging, and with your inner voice as your guide, know that you will find yourself where you belong.

WRAP IT UP

Your ego thinks it knows what's best for you. Once you learn to muffle it, your inner voice will ring loud and clear and help you align your choices with who you truly are and what you need to be fulfilled.

Learning to trust your inner voice as your truth will come with practice, and you'll master this skill by having conviction in your decisions. In doing so, your confidence will grow. You'll be more open and emotionally available to bond with the people around you and ready to take on your last lessons of preparation.

The first five steps of this process have focused on creating a self-loving, healthy, optimistic, less-stressed, more in-tune you to support your change. With these attributes as a larger part of you, you're well-conditioned for what's next. Having support from others is one of the most important elements of successfully making changes, so you'll conclude Part Two by learning the necessity of connecting with and gathering strength from the group of good people surrounding you.

DO THE WORK

- Are you familiar with your inner voice? If so, think and write about how it expresses itself to you and how you can tell the difference between your inner voice and your ego.

- Do you trust your gut feelings enough to use them when you're trying to make good choices? If not, work to actively hear and use your inner voice each day to help you make decisions.

- Notice and record when your inner voice speaks to you, without engaging it. These can be some of the most valuable directions of all.

CHAPTER NINE

STEP 6: GET SUPPORT AND BE TRUE TO YOURSELF

Instead of gathering my friends and family around me for support as I became overwhelmed at work, struggled to be a good mother, and felt my marriage begin to deteriorate, I pushed it all down and glossed it over. I hid the truth from them. I didn't want to bother or burden them. I wanted them to think everything was fine, and I didn't want them to see me as flawed and broken, which was how I felt.

They were the very group with which I should have shared my pain and sense of failure. I clung to the raw emotion instead of having them wrap their love around me. It took me years to learn from this and connect with them in a deeper way, so I could finally draw upon their strength and support and give it openly in return.

I want this to resonate with you at the highest level so you can appreciate how badly we need a network of real people and honest, caring relationships around us to thrive, especially as we're going through significant changes. Leaning on others is not a sign of weakness. You are honoring their love for you by accepting it and making them feel needed and loved in return.

We'll underscore the importance of support on this step and have you take a hard look at your current network. You need to build your personal team with the right individuals to help you through change. You'll need to create new, meaningful relationships as you deepen the ones you have, and let yourself be vulnerable so you can live your life, loving who you are.

BENEFITS TO BEING SUPPORTED

There are serious benefits to having a support system. It builds you up during difficult times and gives you the strength to keep going. It's vital to have a varied group of people with different backgrounds and points of view, so you're covered on the four main types of social support (emotional, affirmational, instrumental, and informational) we as humans need.

Emotional supporters are there as a shoulder to lean or cry on and are important when we're stressed or lonely. Affirmational supporters offer messages that help us believe in ourselves and promote positive self-evaluation, like expressions of confidence or encouragement. Instrumental supporters take care of physical needs and offer a helping hand, and informational supporters provide mentoring and advice, and assist in reducing our anxiety when we have problems that need a solution. Your closest family and most cherished friends may provide all four depending on the situation, and others may specifically provide one or two.

There are health benefits to having a support network that should not be ignored. Their influence can lead you to start and continue healthy habits such as eating well and exercising. They can also encourage you to stop doing unhealthy things like smoking or excessive drinking and even help you avoid relationships that don't work for you.

Knowing you have people who care for you can reduce your stress; seeing others go through the same struggles as you can make them seem less daunting. Being surrounded by individuals who are having the same experiences and trying to attain the same goals can bring you support, empathy, and, most importantly, motivation. Having these bonds as you plan and carry out your changes will enhance your ability to follow through and finish.

BUILD YOUR TEAM OF SUPPORTERS

Who is already on your personal pep squad? Who can you talk to that you trust implicitly and feel safe telling them your deepest fears and wants? It may be only one person right now, and that's fine. Tell them about the changes you're considering and know they'll back you up.

You need to start expanding your network. You'll want it in place by the time you finish your plan and formally commit to it by letting your network know about it. Build yourself a team of people who will bolster you and not question you in making changes.

Friends and family are a great place to start. Just be sure they don't inadvertently transfer their own roadblocks or fears to you. Be choosey where you can; make certain they aren't naysayers and don't bring their own personal agenda to your world, because they may not share your wants or needs.

Have honest, upfront conversations with family about your need for their support without judgment. Tell them you understand they may not agree with your choices for change, but you're asking them to support you, not your decisions (which are yours to make). Let them know you love and appreciate them, but be prepared to set healthy boundaries if necessary.

Your best supporters will be like-minded and like-hearted

and encourage you to express your needs and explore all possibilities. Here, on the landing of your staircase, is where it's vital to gather those supporters. If being motivated and held accountable to your plan by someone outside of your family or social circle resonates with you, consider working with a life coach or another professional. Some women do well with the positive pressure that comes from adding an outsider to their team, and this can give you extra incentive to stick to your plan.

Connecting with people who have successfully gone through similar changes can help build your confidence before you take action. They may have crucial advice to offer, and you can learn from their challenges and understand what it took for them to get through it. Marvel in their success and draw upon their positive energy, keeping in mind that their solutions and path are uniquely theirs; resist the urge to follow too closely in their footsteps instead of sticking with your plan.

SAY GOODBYE TO THOSE WHO GO

Know that your group may shift during this process. In making big changes, there may be people who get left behind because they're part of a job, circle, or situation that no longer serves you. Lovingly say goodbye in person when you can and wish them well; if that's not possible, come to terms with their absence and be grateful for what they taught you or brought to your life.

If there's sadness in letting people go, sit with it and process through it by writing or talking about it instead of suppressing it. It will linger or pop back up in some strange way if you don't work through it. Once you've properly made your peace and have appropriately mourned the loss, you'll have created healthy space within you to welcome new folks into your circle.

BE GOOD WITH BEING YOU

Share your real self and be loved. I intimately understand that allowing yourself to be vulnerable can be frightening, because you're opening yourself up to being judged, rejected, and possibly hurt. But you can't wait for your life to be perfect before letting the world see you.

Being vulnerable can be hard, and even more so if you've experienced disappointment, heartbreaking loss, or profound sadness and have created coping mechanisms to avoid the same pain in the future. Unfortunately, these coping mechanisms often mean you steer clear of making meaningful connections and tend to seal your feelings and your true self inside of you. In another scenario, you might not have learned how to be vulnerable when you were younger, or you may just be a little rusty with being yourself so openly and fearlessly.

The idea of being open about anything personal left me cold

as my 30s gave way to my 40s, and I absorbed the crushing anxiety and crippling self-doubt that came with a failed marriage, my parents' injuries and illnesses, and the changing tide of our company. I was interacting with everyone, but I wasn't sharing myself and my energy, and because I was closed off, they weren't sharing with me either. I felt alone, and there were days when I struggled to get out of the house.

Whether it was my life in pictures on social media or in private with my closest friends, I wore a mask that said, "All is well and I'm too busy to really talk to you." I was hellbent on not letting the real me peek out from behind it, and I buried myself in my work to stay hidden. I had become so good at stuffing everything down that when my unchecked emotion leaked out, people were genuinely surprised.

I've learned to be vulnerable again, to post pictures, share my writing, and even seek out new friends. I'm so incredibly energized, and I try to encourage and empower as many other women as possible to do the same. Know that the reward of living your true and connected life far outweighs the risk of being hurt.

If you don't put yourself out there and try, you'll never really know what you're capable of. Getting comfortable with being vulnerable prepares you to take risks and to make changes more confidently. Regardless of your past or how you're living now, you can work to become more vulnerable.

3 STEPS TO GETTING COMFORTABLE WITH BEING VULNERABLE:

1. Start small. Do easy things that push you outside of your comfort zone and realize you'll survive doing them. Start a conversation with someone you don't know or reconnect with someone you haven't talked to for some time. Take small chances and be vulnerable each day. It may feel a little scary at first, but stick with it and congratulate yourself on your effort.

2. Get comfortable with sharing your feelings. First, tell the ones you trust the most how much you love and respect them. Next, let yourself be openly proud of your accomplishments and express it. Once these acts become easier to do, challenge yourself to calmly, from a place of personal strength, tell people when they have hurt you.

3. Learn not to shy away from situations by getting familiar and more secure with how being vulnerable feels to you. It can show up like an achy heartbreak, pressure, or pit in your stomach. Just like your inner voice, how and where you sense your vulnerability is unique to you, and it gets easier to work through the more you acknowledge it. Take a deep breath and know you can handle any outcome, even if you temporarily feel hurt or exposed.

Your final goal is to courageously do the things that line up with who you are deep down. Say what you want to say, not what you think everyone else wants to hear. Get comfortable talking about how you feel and sharing what you truly need. Then ask for help and graciously accept it.

LIVE AN INTEGRATED, AUTHENTIC LIFE

Feeling the need to hide parts of you can make it seem like you're living multiple lives and leaves you mentally and emotionally weary. Being unclear about who you are and what you really want leads to decisions that don't revolve around what you need to be happy. The power you gain by being at peace with yourself and showing up exactly as you are will change your world.

Living authentically means you're closely aligned with your values, wants, and needs, rather than trying to please others, conform to society's norms, or meet the expectations of important people in your life. Living your authentic life gives you the ability to have genuine and healthier relationships, and it lifts your self-esteem, which can ward off depression. Who really wants to drag around someone else's idea of a good life?

WRAP IT UP

Don't underestimate the power and emotional benefits of having the right people by your side as you begin to imagine your plan for change. The most nurturing and loving members of your circle should be your core supporters. Expand that group so you have multiple layers of overlap, and seek out others who have already made or are in the middle of making similar changes so you can get advice and share a common experience.

Being vulnerable and fully sharing yourself is a huge leap toward living as your authentic self. Preparing to live your life on your own terms is the final piece to being certain about how you want it to look and feel. This will help you get clear on the exact changes you need to make.

These six steps of preparation have laid a foundation of healthful and soulful practices to help you confidently move forward and make changes. Put into regular use the ones that resonate with you, and revisit the ones you did not immediately connect with. In Part Three, you'll learn how to build your plan for change on your strong foundation and stay motivated to reach your goal, so admire your hard work and get ready to finish your climb.

DO THE WORK

- Who is currently in your support network? Is there anyone that brings their own fear or negativity along with their support? Have honest conversations and create healthy boundaries where you need to do so.
- Expand your support team by adding individuals who will lift you up and keep you moving forward. Consider

where you can connect with people who have previously gone through or are currently going through changes that line up with your goals.

- Think and write about how comfortable you are with being vulnerable.
- Work each day to put yourself in situations that allow you to be more vulnerable. Note and write about your feelings and body sensations along with the outcomes. Be proud of your progress.
- Make daily decisions and do the things that allow you to live as close as possible to your values, wants, and needs.

PART THREE

YOUR PLAN
FOR CHANGE

"It takes as much energy to wish as it does to plan."

—ELEANOR ROOSEVELT

CHAPTER TEN

STEP 7: GET UNSTUCK AND CLEAR ON YOUR WHAT, WHY, AND HOW TO CHANGE

The great news about being stuck is that you already know you need to make a change. You just don't know exactly how to go about it, or how to minimize your feelings of fear, anxiety, and even loss that can come with it.

The uncertainty that goes along with change is enough to make us avoid it. Clinging to the comfortable and resisting the unknown keeps us feeling safe, but leaves us living a lackluster life, and certainly not the one we were meant to live. See this as your starting point for the final three stairs of your stairway. The process of moving beyond your safe place is the first foot forward in creating your plan for change.

We'll look at ways to help you get unstuck and decide on the details of your change. Once you're firm on what to change, you'll need to find your motivation and hold on to it. Get clear about why, then explore how in a way that serves you, taking care to avoid challenges like those associated with impostor syndrome, so you don't end up making your life more complicated.

ARE YOU FEELING STUCK?

Does any of this sound familiar to you?

- You feel bad that you can't embrace the jobs, relationships, or careers that seem to go along with other people's expectations, even though you know they don't make you happy.
- You'll feel like a failure or that you can't hack it if you decide to step away from what everyone else seems to have no problem being or doing with a smile.
- You're waiting for divine intervention or secretly wish for some minor catastrophe to bring change.

Don't wait for someone or something to come and change your life. Not living the joy-filled life you were meant to live and feeling regret can be devastating on so many levels.

The power of change, along with the responsibility to carry it through, resides in you.

Change can be scary. Sometimes we just don't have the confidence to know we'll get through it. Give yourself permission to be important enough to take the chance, and then expend the energy to make it happen.

Being stuck and not working your way through it is like the unofficial second definition of insanity. You keep doing the same things over and over, expecting a different result. Maybe you think you'll wake up one day and be fine with everything the way it is?

6 TOOLS TO HELP YOU GET UNSTUCK

The solid foundation of mental and physical wellness you've begun to build will empower you to move yourself forward. Focus your energy on getting beyond the stuck place you're in now by using the preparation we've discussed along with a few new and specific tools.

1. Let go of the past to clear the way for a new future. Are you holding on to how things were, or clutching onto regret that something didn't turn out the way you thought it should? Mourn it if you must, feel the weight and sadness, and then release it. It's a bump in the road

on the way to your new life. Writing about it can be cathartic and help you break that hold.

2. Practicing mindfulness and meditation will help put the past in your rear view so you can find meaning in the way things are now and focus your mental efforts on paving the road ahead.

3. Negative thoughts, feelings, and talk can ball you up and make you hold tight to where you are. They don't give way to the space you need to try something new. Let the positivity in—here's where your optimism will really benefit you. Believe you will make changes and live a life you love, and you will.

4. Be grateful for your strength and the life you have right now; the energy that comes from it will help you move to your next phase. Start each day by being thankful for all you have, even for the situation you feel stuck in. It's a stepping stone and going beyond it will lead you to your next, more gratifying step.

5. Lean on your support network. Talking openly with them about feeling stuck may help you unearth solutions. They may also have advice to offer that inspires you.

6. Small changes in your life can create energy for larger ones. Shift your scenery by taking a trip and come back with fresh eyes to see fresh solutions. Alternate the routes you drive each day or move your furniture around and then pay attention. What messages are you getting? What synchronicities are you seeing?

GET CLEAR ON WHAT

Reaching the point where you can no longer stand something is a powerful place for you to be. Your next step is to decide exactly what needs to change, and how you want it to look and feel once you've done it. Ask yourself what change will have the greatest impact on your happiness.

Be specific. If you're not happy with your job, for example, what exactly do you need to change? Do you want the same job with another company? Do you want a different job within the same company? Or do you want to leave your career behind and find a new one? The more exacting you can be about where you want to end up, the closer you'll get to being there.

I knew I could no longer stomach endless meetings about meetings, and that my days needed to center on supporting and nurturing people. By concentrating my efforts on changing my job, I decided I couldn't stay in my company, even if in another position. I soon realized I didn't want to stay in the same industry, either.

I took online tests to figure out what work best suited me based on my personality and my wants. It was an excellent way to get in touch with my values and find my purpose, and it got me here, where I spend each day doing work that I love.

DISCOVER YOUR WHY

Find your motivation to change and hold on to it like you're riding a mechanical bull. Your why will be a guiding light in times of self-doubt. It will give you hope when you find yourself confronted by cynics, or by people in your inner circle with the best intentions but their own fear to contend with. Write down your reason and refer to it often as you move through the process of change; you'll be more likely to get to your destination when you keep your why at the front of your mind.

As you're refining your why, choose to emphasize the positive side and opportunity of change rather than seeing it simply as a way to get out of an unpleasant situation. Instead of wanting a new job because you can't stand the people you work with, for example, be motivated to find a job with a more cohesive team and supportive culture. Or, if you're bored in the career you've been in for most of your life, be motivated to find one that is more stimulating and exciting for you, and lines up more closely with your interests.

I decided to leave my job to be more present (in all ways) while raising my son during his formative years, and to find a way to help people live happier, more fulfilled lives. This never wavered. When the how did not immediately reveal itself, I always came back to the why, and it drove me to keep looking for the answer I needed.

Once I got clear on my reason for change, it was like someone had switched off a light and I needed to get out of a dark room. It no longer made sense to just keep standing there. I exited stage left.

DECIDE ON HOW

You need to be comfortable with the route you decide to take. For each possible scenario, honestly evaluate where you'll end up in addition to the actual costs. Ask yourself what the investment of time and money will be, and the overall impact not only on you, but on the people in your life.

If it doesn't add up, rethink your solution so you can put together a feasible plan that works for you. Be real about this. Understand your finances, create spreadsheets to analyze expenses including your monthly bills and debt, and make schedules so you can see and begin to feel how it might affect you and everyone else in your life. (But don't let everyone else's needs come before yours.)

IMPOSTOR SYNDROME: DON'T OVERCOMPLICATE YOUR LIFE

We are mighty women, capable of great things, but we need to take care not to overcomplicate our lives to prove it. Impostor syndrome is a nasty little secret so many of us quietly carry around. Until I dug into it for this book, I had no idea how much of a thing it really was.

Impostor syndrome, first identified as impostor phenomenon in 1978 by psychologists Dr. Pauline Rose Clance and Dr. Suzanne Imes, makes you feel like you don't deserve your achievements and that they are due to luck, temporary effort, or even chance, rather than from your hard work, qualifications, or intelligence. Ultimately, you feel like a fake and worry that people will find out you are less than all the fabulous things you are. Research has shown that up to 70% of people cope with this at one time or another, but it's primarily women who feel this way.

People who suffer from impostor syndrome tend to exhibit specific patterns of behavior. As you read through these, don't be surprised if you recognize them in yourself. If so, you're not alone. I cried as I read about this, having spent so many years feeling like I was not perfect enough or smart enough, and I could never do enough in a day to really deserve the things I had.

Thank you to Dr. Valerie Young, for her extensive work and book, *The Secret Thoughts of Successful Women: Why Capable People Suffer from the Impostor Syndrome and How to Thrive in Spite of It.* She has identified five major centers of shame associated with failure for people suffering with the syndrome, and they are related to how we personally define our competence. She is the expert on the subject, and if you want to take a deeper dive, her groundbreaking book is the place to do it. I take comfort in the fact that these feelings are a large enough part of the human experience that she has defined and personified them for easy use.

THE 5 COMPETENCE TYPES OF IMPOSTOR SYNDROME

These have been paraphrased with permission and approval from Dr. Valerie Young:

1. Perfectionist: This is about how you go about getting things done. You set standards so high they can almost never be attained by you or anyone else. When you come close, but not 100%, it's a total failure. It's hard to trust anyone else to do things as well as you do.
2. Expert: You place the most importance on how much experience you have or how much you know. You never learn enough to feel like you're fully qualified and continue to seek out certifications or degrees to increase your skills or knowledge. You're afraid you'll be exposed for not knowing everything you should.
3. Soloist: Your focus here is on who is getting things done. (And in your mind, it better be you.) You feel like asking for help is admitting failure, and you should be able to do everything on your own. You have the need to prove your worth by doing it all yourself.

4. Natural Genius: How and when you accomplish things is your concern. You assume you should be able to do something the right way the first time, and if you have to work at it you feel ashamed and like you're a fraud. If you don't or can't do something quickly and easily, even with difficult or complex projects, you feel you have failed.

5. Superwoman: How many things you can handle at once and how well you can do all of them is your measure of success. You push yourself to be outstanding in every role you take on or play (mom, mate, friend, keeper of the home, employee, boss, entrepreneur, volunteer, etc.). You think you should effortlessly succeed in the many facets of your life at the same time, and doing poorly in any of them makes you feel as if you're failing.

OVERCOME IMPOSTOR SYNDROME AND CHOOSE THE RIGHT CHANGES

Whether you recognize yourself in one or all of the types, the results are the same, and this line of thinking can get in the way of making your changes. You may see small parts of a few types in yourself, but there is typically a single supreme type that comes through. Acknowledge the ones you identify with and know they do not define you.

Now that you've done that, how do you avoid the pain and pitfalls of these insecurities so you can make the right changes?

Be kind to yourself and love who you are right now. Take the time to mentally review all you've done and embrace your victories as your own. Realize you have earned and are deserving of where you are, and even more deserving of where you want to go.

Share your thoughts or concerns with your support network and mentors. They can help reassure you that these are very normal feelings that are shared by other equally accomplished people, and give you the love and support you need to push through your personal barriers. Remember, everyone has something they struggle with.

Banish the thought that everything you do must be perfect. Imperfection is not an indicator that you are not good enough or smart enough, and trying to make everything perfect will slow you down or paralyze you. Understand that no one is perfect. Instead, have confidence in your ability to give something your full attention and try your best.

Do not feel the need to get another certification or degree solely because it will validate the fact that you are bright and able. However, if going back to school is a dream you thought you'd never realize, carefully consider it. If it allows you to do something you've always wanted to do and it won't stretch you or your family to the breaking point, go for it.

Use your inner voice to help decide the right next move for

you. If the superwoman inside of you is saying, "I can push through and do this!" but your inner voice is saying, "This is way too much to take on," pay attention to it. Trusting my inner voice and paying attention to the signs helped me avoid a six-figure-plus mistake.

My need to prove to everyone, including myself, that I could apply and get accepted to a graduate program at 46 almost overshadowed my need to spend more, not less, time with my son. I almost forgot that I was trying to make my life easier, not harder.

WRAP IT UP

Deciding to get unstuck will empower you to do the work and get clear on the what, why, and how of making your change. Understand your worth and avoid making your life more difficult with grandiose plans that don't align with the things you truly want and need. Steering clear of impostor syndrome tendencies and listening to your inner voice will not only help you create the right plan that is unique to you and your values, but will also help you forge a path toward your contentment that is easier to travel.

Deciding to formally create and carry out the process of making a significant change can give you seemingly bound-less energy to get started. Building a strong, well-detailed plan that you are responsible for is central to keeping your commitment and enthusiasm high to see it through to the end. The next step (your next-to-last step on your staircase to change) will help you create your specific plan so you can stick to it.

DO THE WORK

- Are you feeling stuck? If so, use the tools presented here and work to get yourself unstuck and ready for change.
- Think and write about what you need to change and be specific.
- What is your motivation to make your change? Think and write about your "why" in positive terms.
- How do you need to make this change so it works for you and the people in your life? Fully analyze the commitment of money and time and the impact it will have on those around you. Adjust your plan if necessary.
- Is impostor syndrome something you've experienced? If so, which of the types do you see in yourself and what is the predominant type?
- If you're being held back by impostor syndrome feelings, write about them, share them with the people you trust, and use your inner voice to help you decide the right way to proceed.

CHAPTER ELEVEN

STEP 8: HOPE IS NOT A STRATEGY, BUT CREATING SMART GOALS IS

How many times have you made well-meaning, yet vague New Year's resolutions to be healthier, get more exercise, or something else aspirational that didn't seem to last? You know the change would have a positive impact on your life, but not putting a serious plan in place to hold yourself accountable turns it into more of a wish or hope, rather than an attainable goal. "Hope is not a strategy" is one of my favorite sayings, borrowed from my previous professional life. (Courtesy of Vince Lombardi, one of the greatest football coaches of all time.)

You've made change important enough to you to read this

book, and you've properly prepared yourself by adopting new healthy practices and exploring mind-expanding approaches. Now you're ready to take a huge step up toward your goal. Make a formal commitment to yourself and imprint your goals on your brain by physically handwriting them. Once you've done that, your next task is to create a detailed plan outlining the actions you need to take to make that change.

You'll learn about SMART goals and use them to create a workable plan that will keep you moving toward your end goal at a lively pace. The more diligent you are in creating this roadmap for yourself, the more productive you will be. Spelling out the details makes you significantly more likely to reach your goals, so get ready to lay it all out for yourself.

4 GOOD REASONS TO HANDWRITE YOUR GOALS

Handwriting your goals will help engrave them in your mind and increase your chances of being successful. Studies show that you are 42% more likely to attain your goals by writing them down rather than keeping them in your head.

Here's why:

1. Writing out your goals is a signal to your brain to memorize them. Your brain remembers something more easily when you're directly involved in creating it rather than just reading it, a phenomenon called the *generation*

effect. Your brain is constantly reviewing information and deciding what's most important to you. So, if you write something down, your mind knows you've decided to focus on it and converts it to memory for storage and retrieval when you need it.

2. Memory also gets stored outside of your brain (part two of the generation effect). The information about your goal gets stored on a piece of paper that can be used as a daily visual reminder. To keep your objectives top of mind, put them where you'll see them on a regular basis. But don't just slap them up on your refrigerator with a magnet from your trip to Washington, DC, only to get lost among the pictures and be forgotten.

3. Writing things down activates both sides of the brain. The left hemisphere is more logic-based, and the right hemisphere is associated with creativity. Bringing both to the process will help you come up with imaginative, reasonable (and do-able) plans to help you hit your goals.

4. The physical act of writing out a goal helps decrease stress by unburdening your brain. Then, if you cross it off once it's completed, it gives your brain a feeling of accomplishment. These good feelings motivate your brain to keep doing or trying new things and keep the positivity flowing.

Move your written goals around so they don't blend in with the background, or put them where you can't avoid looking at them every day. I put things I absolutely must remember in places where I can't help but see them. I tape them on windows and doors and put them on top of my keyboard or right on my computer screen, so there's no chance of me not seeing them first thing in the morning.

I started using a yellow legal pad at work to write out my goals and to-do list when it became too hard to keep them in my head. Once something made it onto that pad of paper, it became a must-do. It was my written contract with myself, and there were times when I had no idea how I was going to accomplish it, but writing it down brought commitment, some good pressure, and, eventually, the way to get it done.

The guys at work gave me guff for always having my yellow pad with me. Interestingly, not long after the appearance of my yellow pad, I started seeing more and more yellow pads on everyone else's desks. My legal pad has since morphed into a smaller steno notebook, but it remains a powerful tool that helps me in both my personal and professional life.

WHAT THE HECK ARE SMART GOALS?

SMART goals may not be the sexiest thing you've ever seen in a self-help book, but using them to make changes so you can live the life you deserve is exciting. The idea first came about in the 1950s, starting with Peter Drucker's Management by Objectives concept. This laid out a process that helped the work of individuals and teams roll up to an organization's overarching plan, through challenging but achievable goals. The first use of the SMART acronym came about in 1981; it helped make the exercise more memorable, and it's still actively used by businesses of all types and by successful people at work and at home.

SMART goals will help you focus your effort, use your time wisely, and stay motivated to make your change. Commit the acronym to memory for use now and every time you set a goal for yourself in the future. It will very quickly become a good habit and a great way to make yourself responsible for getting what you want.

S: SPECIFIC

State your goal and be as specific as possible with the details as to how you're going to achieve it. Let's take the popular New Year's intention of being healthier and expand on it. If your definition and method of being healthier is to work out, set a goal to exercise in a way you enjoy that will raise your heart rate for specific amounts of time per day, at specific times each week. Let's use riding a bike as the exercise for this example.

M: MEASURABLE

Your goals must be quantifiable or measurable. Using our example, a target of riding your bike four times per week for 60 minutes each time can be measured. You'll track your progress as you work up to this goal. You may need to start with ten minutes twice a week and then increase the times per week and minutes per session, but this gets you headed toward your desired result.

A: ATTAINABLE

Avoid setting yourself up for failure by setting challenging goals that are possible for you to reach. For example, if you have bad knees, choosing to run as your way of exercise probably won't be a good method for you. You should also not expect to exercise for 60 minutes, four times per week right off the bat if you've never worked out a day in your life. Make your expectations and goals realistic based on what you can attain by putting in the work.

R: RELEVANT

Your goals should be set by you, for you, based on the things you want in your life. Goals you are not attached to, or that are based on what other people think you should do, will lack your personal investment and energy. Go back to the work you've already done and be clear on what change you want and need to be happy. Your goals should serve as inspiration and motivation to you.

T: TIME DEPENDENT

When do you want to achieve your goal? Make this realistic, but not too far off into the future. If you're working up to riding your bike for 60 minutes, four times per week, start with a reasonable schedule you can build on.

For example, ride your bike for ten minutes, twice a week, for the first two weeks. Schedule your rides first thing in the morning or whatever time is best for you, whenever you are most likely to keep doing it. For the next two weeks, plan to ride for 15 minutes, three times a week, and so on. Build out a plan with increased exercise time and instances per week that can be flexible based on your personal progress and lead you to your goal.

CREATE YOUR SMART GOAL AND PLAN

Use this sentence as a template to create your goal for your change:

I'll (your goal) by (how you'll do your goal). I'll know I'm making progress because (way you'll measure the goal) for (time).

Using our bike riding example, the sentence reads: "I'll be healthier by incorporating regular exercise into my life. I'll exercise by riding my bike. I'll know I'm making progress because I'll work up to bike riding for 60 minutes, four times per week."

Write out your SMART goal and then break it down into time-dependent, measurable, bite-sized pieces, the mini-steps of your plan that will take you to the finish line. Remember to use reasonable time frames, but make sure you also challenge and stretch yourself. Spend the time you need with this process to put together a game plan that excites you and gets you up and out of bed and ready to get after it.

To stay organized, I highly recommend writing out a schedule and timeline using a monthly calendar and putting it with your written goals. It doesn't need to be fancy; you can easily download and print free monthly calendars from multiple websites. I'm a very visual person, so I have an old-fashioned wall calendar hanging in my kitchen, and I handwrite anything time sensitive on it, including goals, tasks, and appointments, to keep them in front of me.

WRAP IT UP

Get your goals out of your head and onto a piece of paper to let your brain know you mean business. This simple act will kick off the processes of memorization, activation, and motivation to help you attain them. Keep them in your eyesight, review them daily, and physically cross them out, check them off, scribble through them—whatever satisfies you most—when you've completed them.

The act of creating and physically writing out SMART goals will increase your likelihood of following through and making that important change you're now ready to make. You get to build the plan based on your wants and needs that will inspire you to become your own success story. You've learned how to turn your desire for change into a bona fide strategy, and now all that is left for you to do is execute it and realize your dreams.

DO THE WORK

- Handwrite your goal for change and put it where you'll easily see it.
- Spend the time you need to create your SMART goal and build out the plan that will help you make your change.
- Write out the schedule and timeline for your plan using a monthly calendar.

CHAPTER TWELVE

STEP 9: STAY MOTIVATED UNTIL YOU CROSS YOUR FINISH LINE

Once I made the decision to be a life coach, I took a series of measured steps to find my way here. I started small, first by discussing my plans with the handful of people I trusted most, and their responses were, "I love that for you," and thankfully, "Of course that's what you're going to do!" It was exactly what I needed to hear.

Second, I wrote a letter to a larger group and expanded my support team, then took a deep breath and went live with a website that gave everyone the opportunity to see and get to know me. I pushed through my perfectionist tendencies, designed the layout, and wrote the copy in under a month.

It was frightening at first, and then incredibly invigorating to be out there in the world in that way.

I then called upon the tools you've studied here, created SMART goals using my steno pad of accountability, and kept my personal pep squad in the loop about the good and the bad. At that point, I moved from doing to being, and I emerged as the woman I finally knew I could be. Now it's your turn.

TAKE ONE LAST LOOK BACK

Let's look at how far you've come and all you've accomplished. You've laid a foundation of physical and mental health and have learned to trust your inner voice to help guide you. You're being true to yourself and have made real connections with more people to expand your personal support group in preparation of the change you're about to make.

Maybe you were stuck and have moved beyond it, but now you're crystal clear about your personal why for making this change. You've created a solid plan using goals that will help you hold yourself accountable. It's now time for you to go the last mile, which is yours and yours alone. Take your last step and finish this magnificent journey you've started.

PRACTICE WELL-BEING, NOW MORE THAN EVER

Continue to expand on the healthy practices you've added to your life. Change, even with its long-term benefits, can be stressful while you're in the midst of it. Eating and sleeping well and getting your heart rate up will help you guard against stress and keep your vibrations way up high, and being optimistic will set a spirited tone of can-do positivity.

Start each day with gratitude for who you are and what you've accomplished. Be thankful for your courage and the fact that you've set your sights on this change you absolutely must make. Appreciate the people you've always had by your side, along with the new ones who have come into your life to support you in this.

Seek peace and bolster your confidence by using the practices of mindfulness and meditation. Incorporate them into your daily routine, even in small ways. Imagine the positive feelings you'll have when this process is complete and the joy you'll have generated with your own actions.

PUT YOURSELF FIRST FOR NOW

Keep your non-essential activities to a minimum, like meeting friends for mid-morning coffee or lunch during the week, so you can focus on your plan and what needs to be done each day until you reach your goal. It's too easy for something to catch your attention and pull you off course, especially if you're feeling stuck or challenged. Try to avoid interruptions and give your precious time and energy to yourself first, and then to the people and things that deserve it most—*after* you.

Work to minimize your distractions. Whether it's family, friends calling or texting, the television, or social media, put up a mental (and physical, if necessary) "Do Not Disturb" sign during very specific hours so you can focus on the task at hand. Find a space to dedicate to your work. If you can't do it at home, commit to finding a place nearby that you can easily access when you need to.

Use your ultimate goal and your why as constant motivation. Write them out together, put them where you can see them, and read them every day. They will serve as your ongoing inspiration and remind you why this change is so important to you.

MAKE A PLAN FOR EACH DAY

Plan your activities for each day either the night before or first thing in the morning, so you know what you need to do. Get in the mode of setting aside five to ten minutes at the same time each day and spell out exactly what you need to accomplish and when. Add any outside commitments so you can schedule accordingly, and be realistic about what you can get done in the day.

My power hour falls somewhere between 7 and 9 a.m., when I have giant bursts of mental clarity and creativity. The last thing I want is to use that energy and time to make lists and set a schedule. To avoid holding myself back in the morning, I take the end of each day to honestly review the steno pad to see what has and has not been done, without judgment.

Because of that productive period in the morning, I write out my schedule in the evening, including my to-do list and appointment times for the next day. That way, if I wake up or jump out of the shower with something on my mind that absolutely needs to be expressed, I already have the blueprint for the day. This helps me avoid feeling like I'm behind or have to play catch-up just to set up the day.

CELEBRATE SUCCESSES, SHARE STRUGGLES, AND ADJUST AS NEEDED

Create small goals in your overall plan and congratulate yourself for reaching them. Set up a positive feedback loop that keeps you moving forward and luxuriate in the feeling of getting things done. Physically cross items off your list when they're completed so your brain gets the full satisfaction and enjoyment of accomplishing each one, and let it feed on the good vibes of your success.

Be proud of the work you do and the goals you achieve, even the small ones. Take time to recognize your personal victories along the way, and allow the positivity of each completed task to build momentum and carry you forward. Create specific rewards for yourself, like dinner out with your biggest fan-friends, or a purchase that goes hand in hand with your change—things that reinforce the well-supported, well-crafted life you are building.

Make verbal commitments to yourself and others by talking about the change you'll be making, the steps you need to take to get there, and when you plan to take them. Openly share your progress and lean on your people in times of doubt. Include your best supporters on your personal wins and celebrations, as they can be an added layer of positivity and accountability.

At the end of each week, thoroughly review your plan and the headway you've made, so you can take inventory of what's working and what's not. Allow yourself to be flexible when necessary and decide what tweaks need to be made. Be kind to yourself through this process. Remember the objective is to make the change you've committed to, not to rigidly follow the plan you've created.

Make adjustments along the way, but don't stop. You've come entirely too far to do that.

ACT AS IF AND BELIEVE

Early in my career, I found myself surrounded primarily by very smart men with light-years more experience than I had. I was thrust into business situations that I was hardly prepared for as a twenty-something woman, new to the wine scene. So I watched them closely and learned to project confidence and imitate their competence, because I knew I would eventually figure it out.

This ties in with the "act as if" approach, where you present yourself in a way that makes it seem like the thing you want to become, or the change you want to make, is already a part of you. Acting-as-if falls flat without optimism, the hard work you've already done to prepare yourself, and a plan to get there. Using this approach confirms you're ready for what's next and allows your brain to have a dress rehearsal for the things that are to come.

As much as you can, look like, act like, and feel like you've already accomplished your grand feat of change. Start with an infectious smile and share it. Walk and carry yourself with the confidence of a person who has completed their personal mission, and dress like you have, too.

WRAP IT UP

Being healthy and positive, creating the right space and time for your work, plus discipline through daily planning will keep you on track for your last push forward. Set smaller, attainable goals to celebrate to keep you motivated. Invite and encourage your support team to be fully invested in your success, share your triumphs and temporary setbacks with them, and soak up their support every chance you get.

Your plan, like you, is changeable; be forgiving and adjust it when you need to. Play the part of a person who has already been transformed by acting, dressing, and projecting your personal happiness as you move toward your finish line. Get to the end, make the change, and be grateful for your strength and those who helped you.

DO THE WORK

- Your well-being is more important now than ever. Be healthy and energized; make yourself a priority so you can attain your goal.
- Focus on the work you need to do by making the time and creating the right space to do it. Temporarily suspend non-essential activities until you reach your goal.
- Write out a plan of action for each day, either the night before or first thing in the morning.
- Set smaller goals in your plan that are easy to attain and applaud your achievements.
- Be open with your support network about the details of your plan, and share your highs and lows with them.
- Review your progress at the end of each week and adjust

your plan when necessary. Show yourself kindness as you do.

- Act as if you've already made your change and keep working until you do.

CHAPTER THIRTEEN

TIE IT ALL TOGETHER AND TRANSFORM YOURSELF

The imaginary truck of change—the one you hope will hit you on your way to work so you don't have to deal with the nonsense there, or maybe get you on the way home so you can have a mini-vacation of sorts—is not coming for you. You know deep down it would not give you the relief you want; it would only bring a cyclone of chaos, and you don't need that. Now that you've finished this book and have substantial tools to help you, be empowered to change lanes on your own terms and leave that truck behind.

This book was written to inspire you to action and teach you how to change your life. With effort, you'll be properly prepared and readier than ever to be the real you, open to being truly supported, and have a method to make yourself responsible for what you want. Decide not to stay still a single day longer. Start changing your life today.

REPETITION IS THE MOTHER OF LEARNING

I used a rule of threes in my previous business life to communicate important information to salespeople and managers. As demands increased and everyone's days became more hectic, it seemed they needed to read, be told, or be shown something at least three times before they could "hear" it. I took notice and repeated messages multiple times in various ways to help them become a more permanent part of the team's mind and move them to action.

Take this same approach with the things you've learned in this book that must become part of you and what you do. Create mental, visual, and verbal reminders to stitch them into the fabric of your days, and do them with such regularity they move from repeated action to habit. To this end, let's review the interconnected steps you've taken on the way to your transformation before you finish this book and close these chapters to start new ones of your own.

PART ONE: INSPIRATION

Seek inspiration through the extraordinary experiences of others and have faith in your ability to make changes.

Through inspirational stories, know you'll be rewarded for your work and that a life of struggle can become a story of great personal success with the switch of a lane.

PART TWO: PREPARATION

Step 1

Bringing self-love to your journey may be one of the most significant steps for you to take. Having a safe place to write or journal gives you a haven for reflection and expression and is a good starting place to explore where you want to finish. Give yourself grace to set the tone for your work, and move yourself toward the top of your list, where you need to be.

Step 2

Once your self-love is flowing, you'll be more open to making yourself a priority and committing time in your day to concentrate on you. Create an organized space around you and build yourself a solid base of health and balance by feeding your body with healthy foods and getting enough sleep. Exercise to get your heart rate up, even in small spurts, to perk up your confidence and give you a general feeling of well-being. Be grateful each morning to start the day on a positive note.

Step 3

With your self-regard and health on an upswing, positivity and optimism can reign supreme in your life and spill over into your thoughts, feelings, and interactions. This, along with actively working to keep your vibrational energy and overall happiness level high, will help you attract the things you want through the Law of Attraction. Be ready to see synchronous cues and signs showing you the right way to proceed, and listen to what the universe is telling you, regardless of how the message is received.

Step 4

Having connected to the energy and guidance of the universe, you're ready to learn the life-changing practices of mindfulness and meditation. Their stress and anxiety-reducing abilities are only the start; by diminishing your self-judgment, they also encourage you to have more love for yourself and be ready to accept it from those around you. Using these practices to unwind your mind will give you room to fully explore your potential and open yourself up to the possibilities change can bring.

Step 5

The tools of mindfulness and meditation will put you in the right frame of mind and give you the ability to connect with your inner voice and distinguish it from your ego. Your ego exists to protect you, but it can also keep you from making changes because it thinks you're safer staying where you are.

Your inner voice knows what you truly need, and with a little practice you can recognize it and call upon it to help guide you. Your belief in your ability to make the right decisions will grow and fully blossom once you trust the advice your inner voice is giving.

Step 6

By the time you've taken the last five considerable steps to strengthen yourself, you'll be ready to build a team of loving and caring individuals to support you. In addition to the right members of your family, friends, and network, specifically seek out people who have gone or are currently going through the same experiences. Allow yourself to be you, and work in small ways each day to become more comfortable with being vulnerable. Put yourself out there and understand the power of making changes and living a life based on your wants and needs.

PART THREE: YOUR PLAN FOR CHANGE

Step 7

With your inspired spirit, prepared body and mind, and a group gathered around you for support, you'll feel fully equipped to take on your change. Focus your attention and activity on moving beyond being stuck, and use the energy from making small adjustments in your everyday life to help you push through it. Do the mental work so you're clear on what to change, understand and hold tight to your why (which is your motivation), and then decide how to go about it. Avoid overcomplicating your life with changes that feed the hurt places living inside of you, like the shame centers associated with impostor syndrome. They will not serve you.

Step 8

Once you're clear on the specific details of your change, the simple act of writing down your goals and reading them on a regular basis will make you much more likely to reach them. Handwriting this information tells your brain this is important to you and should be memorized. Putting together a well-thought-out plan that is SMART (Specific, Measurable, Attainable, Relevant to you, and Time dependent), will help you focus and be accountable to your goals for change.

Step 9

Take everything you've learned in this process, make a point of putting yourself first, keep your distractions to a minimum, and give your final push the focus it needs. Create a plan of action for each day, review your progress each week, and adjust your master plan when needed. Keep your support network close, celebrate small victories to keep your motivation high, and act as if you've already attained your goals until you have.

BECOME YOUR OWN SUCCESS STORY OF CHANGE

Harness the power within you, knock down your walls of self-doubt, and transform yourself into the person you've only wished you could be. You've made it to the top of your stairway. On the brink of greatness, take stock of the things you've learned, and use them to firmly move yourself into your greatest and most fulfilling life. It's waiting for you!

Be a brilliant beacon of inspirational light and let your strength and determination shine. With your newfound confidence, spread the word to other women you see struggling, and let them know it's not supposed to be this hard. Join their circle of support, and through your example as a heroine of change, amplify their ability to do the same.

This book exists to help you foster connection and create community around your change. Please share your stories of triumph with me, or let me know where you're stuck. We'll celebrate your wins, and as a member of your extended support team, I can help you through the hard parts, too.

ACKNOWLEDGMENTS

I am thankful for my foundational group of women including my family, my oldest and dearest friends, mentors, co-workers, and the extraordinary women I've met and worked with over the past few years. Your support and stories have given me encouragement and strength.

I am forever grateful to Vinnie Batiato for insisting that I put myself near the top of my list of people to care for. Your patience and love have helped me through some of the most challenging years of my life, and your support of this great adventure has been nothing short of spectacular.

Thank you, Lisa Vakulin-Rose and Amy Zimmerman, for your unwavering belief in me. You had no doubt in my abilities from the very beginning, and your overwhelmingly positive response to my writing gave me the confidence to keep going to the end.

I am so incredibly fortunate and grateful for having connected with my editor, Danielle Anderson. I said early on that my book would be better because of you, and your suggestions and insistence to dig deeper helped me to be thorough and even more open and honest in my work.

I may not have pushed through my perfectionist tendencies to write this book had it not been for the work of Dr. Valerie Young. Thank you, Dr. Young, for giving me permission to include the competence types of impostor syndrome from your book. They helped me put a name and face to my own struggles and recognize that I was not suffering alone. By sharing them here, I want them to do the same for even more women.

A final thanks to Dennis Styck for taking a chance on me, an unknown girl in the wine world who grew up loving Jimi Hendrix, too.

Made in the USA
Las Vegas, NV
16 September 2021

30375102R00104